EASY KETO DESSERTS

60+ Low-Carb, High-Fat Desserts for Any Occasion

Carolyn Ketchum

VICTORY BELT PUBLISHING

Las Vegas

First Published in 2018 by Victory Belt Publishing Inc.

ISBN-13: 978-1-628602-92-0

Front Cover Photography by Hayley Mason and Bill Staley

Cover Design by Justin-Aaron Velasco

Interior Design by Yordan Terziev and Boryana Yordanova

Printed in Canada

TC 0118

CONTENTS

PREFACE: HOW SWEET IT IS

I just spent the past three months of my life writing a dessert cookbook. You know what that means? That means I ate a lot of desserts. And if this were any regular old dessert cookbook, it would probably also mean that I gained at least a few pounds. But I didn't. Not even an ounce. And that, my friend, is the magic of *Easy Keto Desserts*.

Admittedly, I didn't eat all of these desserts on my own. I shared with my family, and I gave much of it away to my friends and neighbors. I was a really popular gal for a while there, leaving cakes and cookies and tarts on doorsteps all over the neighborhood. But still, as a good recipe creator, I tasted and tested, and I tasted and tested again. There was no shortage of sweet keto treats passing these lips over the past few months. And I wouldn't have it any other way.

Chances are good, however, that you don't cook and bake for a living like I do. You don't have time to taste and test, and taste and test again. When you want something sweet, you want it *yesterday*. You have no need of complicated cakes and multistep desserts that require any number of obscure and hard-to-find ingredients. You prefer simple and straightforward, but you still want something that will wow your carb-loving friends. You want easy, but you don't want it to taste like it.

That's where *Easy Keto Desserts* comes in. With this cookbook, I have taken all the guesswork out of making fabulous ketogenic desserts. This is my passion, people! I sincerely love nothing more than sharing delectable low-carb, high-fat dessert recipes and making the keto lifestyle that much more enjoyable—and that much more accessible, too. Because when we know we can have a wee indulgence at the end of the day, one that doesn't wreak havoc on our hard work and progress, keto suddenly doesn't seem so hard after all.

It's long been my mission to prove to the world that the ketogenic diet need not be boring or restrictive. I am not really the sort of person to toot my own horn—oh, who am I kidding? Toot toot!—but I flatter myself that I have exceeded this goal. With *Easy Keto Desserts*, the evidence is in and the jury has reached a verdict. Keto is easy, delicious, and anything but boring.

Grab a fork, my friend, and dig in. Because you can have your keto cake and eat it, too. Just as long as you save me a bite.

INTRODUCTION:
MY DIET AND DESSERT PHILOSOPHY

I have a sweet tooth, and I am not afraid to use it. I firmly believe that being able to have a healthy dessert is part of what helps me stay the course on my ketogenic diet. And since my dessert recipes are among the most popular recipes on my website, *All Day I Dream About Food,* I know that many of you feel the same way.

It's been said many times that the keto diet is not about deprivation; you shouldn't always be hungry, and you shouldn't feel like you are consigned to eating bacon and eggs day in and day out. There could be worse fates, of course, but that kind of restriction gets tiresome pretty quickly. Many people find themselves struggling to stick with keto after a few months because they aren't quite sure how to make it interesting. The ability to indulge a little here and there can make this way of eating a lot more fun and a lot more livable. For many of us, that can be the difference between using keto as a temporary quick fix or sticking with it as a long-term healthy lifestyle.

Some people choose to avoid sweets altogether, and that is their prerogative. We all find our own way here, and we have to choose our own paths. There is an overwhelming amount of advice out there, and it can be hard to make sense of it all. But the reality is that there is no single "right way" to do a ketogenic diet. No one can tell you exactly how to make it work for you. If being abstemious and giving up sweets entirely is your approach, I am all for it. But if you purchased this book, then chances are you want a little dessert, at least once in a while. Welcome to the club.

A ketogenic diet is a wonderful tool for conquering cravings and breaking old and ingrained habits. But that doesn't have to mean taking all the enjoyment out of eating. No matter which diet you're on, food should be fun, and eating should be pleasurable. Food is such a defining aspect of our society. It's more than just sustenance: it's family, it's community, and it's celebration. And what is more celebratory than enjoying a luscious dessert that doesn't derail your healthy efforts?

But let's not go overboard. You may not like to hear it, but portion control is important, even when it comes to keto desserts. People are sometimes surprised to hear me, the Keto Baking Queen, advocate for moderation. But just think about it: while a single keto brownie might fit in perfectly with your macros, the whole pan of brownies will not. It's just simple math. And if you eat keto sweets for breakfast, lunch, and dinner, you are doing so to the exclusion of other healthy nutrients.

My personal approach is to keep dessert as dessert. That means eating a reasonable portion after dinner. Although I do eat some dessert almost every day, there are times when I've filled myself up so much on steak and broccoli that I can't manage more than a few bites of dessert—just enough to make that sweet tooth sing!

If you find that you struggle with portion control, I recommend a few approaches. First, consider my small-batch recipes that make only two to four servings, so portion control is built right in. If you do choose to make a bigger recipe, rely on your freezer as a way to portion out the leftovers. And make a large dessert only when you have the opportunity to share it and give much of it away. Friends, neighbors, and coworkers are often appreciative of your efforts, and hey, maybe this will help them discover the keto diet, too!

It's a sugar-filled world out there, and temptation is all around us. I say why not fight fire with fire?

It's a Piece of Cake! (Or as Easy as Pie)

The wonderful part about desserts is that they have universal appeal, irrespective of how much time and effort they take to make. In fact, some of the simplest desserts are the ones that look the most appetizing. Fancy cakes that look like castles or cookies that resemble snow globes are certainly beautiful to behold, but I find that I don't much care to eat them. In my experience, they never taste quite as good as they look, and I am inevitably disappointed.

The reality is that you don't need to be a pastry chef to make beautiful desserts. Creating sweet treats should be fun, not stressful, and I want you to be able to enjoy the process as much as the end results. The recipes in this book use simple techniques that any home baker can easily master. There's nothing intimidating here, nothing overly complicated—just easy, creative, and mouthwatering recipes. When dessert is stress-free, it's that much tastier.

Keep in mind that *simple* is not necessarily synonymous with *fast*. Nor is the lack of baking or a short ingredient list a good indicator of how easy or quick a recipe is. Sometimes no-bake recipes can take hours to set properly, whereas some baked goods can be consumed shortly after being removed from the oven. You will find recipes of every sort in *Easy Keto Desserts*. Some of these desserts are baked, while others require no baking. You may have to leave some alone for a while, while others you can dig into right away. But all of them are simply delicious.

That's the way the keto cookie crumbles.

KETO DESSERT
ESSENTIALS

The recipes in this book are easy. Period. But in the keto dessert world, recipes frequently call for alternative ingredients that behave very differently from the conventional ingredients you may be familiar with. This is particularly true of flour and sugar substitutes. If you attempt to treat them like wheat flour and sugar, they will defy you out of sheer spite. So it behooves me to take a moment to go over some key points about how best to use these ingredients.

Weigh Your Flours and Nut Meals

Wouldn't it be nice if everyone all over the world measured every ingredient the same way? That doesn't look like it's going to happen any time soon. I am very accustomed to using U.S. volume measurements, like cups and tablespoons, but I fully recognize that they are not always the most accurate. For most ingredients, volume measurements are fine, but keto flours and meals, particularly almond flour and coconut flour, vary quite a bit from brand to brand. Weighing these ingredients can be more accurate and produce better results.

For example, I weighed my Bob's Red Mill almond flour by the cup numerous times and found that it can vary between 97 and 105 grams. I split the difference and used 100 grams; it is the most useful weight since it can easily be divided into half cups and quarter cups. Bob's Red Mill coconut flour typically came out to 110 grams per cup.

When you see gram weights included for these key ingredients, I do recommend that you get out your kitchen scale and weigh them. If you do not own a scale, the next-best option is to use the brands of flours and meals that I use (Bob's Red Mill), and to measure them using the scoop-and-level method. I always use that method when measuring by cups and tablespoons, and you should, too.

FINE-TUNE WHEN NEEDED

Even when you take care to measure as accurately as possible, the variances between brands can throw a recipe off somewhat. Some brands of flour, for example, are more finely ground or more absorbent than others. Be ready to adjust slightly if you need to. Look for cues in the recipe as to what your dough or batter should look like. Should it be scoopable or pourable? Should you be able to roll it into balls easily? Does the recipe state that it should look like "coarse crumbs" or "fine crumbs"? All of these are helpful clues in knowing when to make an adjustment and add a little more flour or a little more liquid or oil.

Always add the additional flour or liquid by the tablespoon, stirring after each addition to see what the batter or dough does before you add more. Coconut flour is extremely absorbent, so a tablespoon can thicken a batter significantly. For small-batch recipes, sometimes even a teaspoon is enough to get the consistency you are looking for.

Familiarize Yourself with Keto Sweeteners

Obviously, we can't have a discussion about keto desserts without discussing low-carb sugar substitutes. And with the dizzying array of alternative sweeteners on the market today, this can be a confusing discussion at times. You may be hoping that I will tell you which sweetener is the absolute, hands-down best one on the planet, but I can't do that. Too much of it comes down to personal preference.

What I can do, however, is give you a little insight into which sweeteners behave the most like sugar in keto sweets and baked goods. Because while there are plenty of great sweetener choices out there, they don't all work the same way. It all comes down to bulk.

BULK VERSUS NON-BULK SWEETENERS

When I say "bulk sweetener," I am not referring to buying large quantities of sweetener from a bin at your local health food store. In this case, the term *bulk* refers to whether the sweetener itself has weight and volume. A bulk sweetener will add to the volume, or "bulk," of a recipe and thus will affect its consistency, which may be critical to its success.

Some sweeteners, like stevia and monk fruit extract, simply sweeten things. A mere ½ teaspoon of either one can sweeten an entire cake that serves twelve people. Obviously, though, concentrated sweeteners such as these will add nothing in terms of volume and won't do anything for the texture or consistency of your dessert.

Sweeteners like erythritol and xylitol have significant bulk, as well as a crystalline structure similar to sugar. They measure more like sugar, they add volume and affect consistency, and hence they behave more like sugar. They can make the difference between a cake that deflates after baking and one that stays risen, or a pudding that sets and one that remains a puddle of goo.

That all sounds simple enough, right? Right, but then there's the fact that erythritol by itself is only about 70 percent as sweet as sugar, so you need to add *more* of it to make up the difference in sweetness, which could also affect the consistency of a recipe. Xylitol is about as sweet as sugar, but it comes with its own issues; it tends to raise blood sugar a little more than erythritol and can cause serious gastric upset when consumed in large quantities. It's also highly toxic to dogs even in minute amounts. I no longer use xylitol in my recipes.

Adding even more to the confusion are all the different sweetener blends on the market these days. These usually combine two or more alternative sweeteners, and more of them seem to crop up on a daily basis. Some of them are as sweet as sugar, some are more concentrated, and all of them are aiming to get their share of your pocketbook. Which is why so much of it comes down to personal preference.

Have I confused you yet? Don't worry, I promise it's not as bad as it sounds.

My preference is Swerve, an erythritol blend that also includes oligosaccharides—a sweet-tasting fiber similar to inulin—to make it measure exactly like sugar. I created and tested all of the recipes in this book using Swerve, and I highly recommend it as one of the best sugar replacements out there. If you choose to substitute another sweetener, I cannot always guarantee the results. That said, xylitol and other erythritol blends that measure like sugar can often be substituted without a loss of taste or texture. And some recipes don't rely on bulk at all for consistency; for those recipes you can use any sweetener your heart desires.

If you do choose to use a non-bulk sweetener, like stevia, monk fruit, or even sucralose, you will need to do a little conversion to attain the correct sweetness. Most brands clearly state how sweet their product is relative to sugar and how to adjust recipes accordingly. For example, Lakanto monkfruit extract has a little conversion chart right on the package, and the SweetLeaf stevia website features a nice conversion calculator for all of its products.

The long and short of it is that sometimes you can make substitutions and sometimes you can't. Wherever possible, I have noted those recipes in which substitutions can be made, and the best sweetener choices. You will find this information in a feature called "Sweetener Options."

INGREDIENTS AND TOOLS

In keeping with the easy theme, the majority of the recipes in this book use fairly standard keto ingredients, as well as everyday cookware and bakeware, most of which can be purchased at regular stores. With the explosive growth of special diets like gluten-free, Paleo, and low-carb, items like almond flour, coconut oil, and alternative sweeteners are no longer just the purview of health food and natural foods stores—which is great news for keto dessert lovers.

Keto Dessert Staples

These are the items I have in my pantry and fridge at all times so I can make dessert whenever the mood strikes.

IN THE FRIDGE:

HEAVY WHIPPING CREAM

CREAM CHEESE

BUTTER
(salted and unsalted)

EGGS (LARGE)

IN THE PANTRY:

BAKING POWDER

VANILLA EXTRACT

BAKING SODA

COCOA POWDER

UNSWEETENED CHOCOLATE (100% CACAO)

FINELY GROUND BLANCHED ALMOND FLOUR
(I recommend Bob's Red Mill)

KETO SWEETENER(S) OF CHOICE
(see pages 13 and 14)

COCONUT FLOUR
(I recommend Bob's Red Mill)

CREAMY PEANUT BUTTER
(unsweetened)

SALT

Dairy-Free Substitutions

If you're dairy-free, or even if you're not, stock up on these great dairy replacements. I always keep avocado oil and coconut oil around, as well as canned coconut milk. And Kite Hill is by far the best brand of dairy-free cream cheese I've found, with the best flavor and consistency and exactly the same carb count as regular cream cheese.

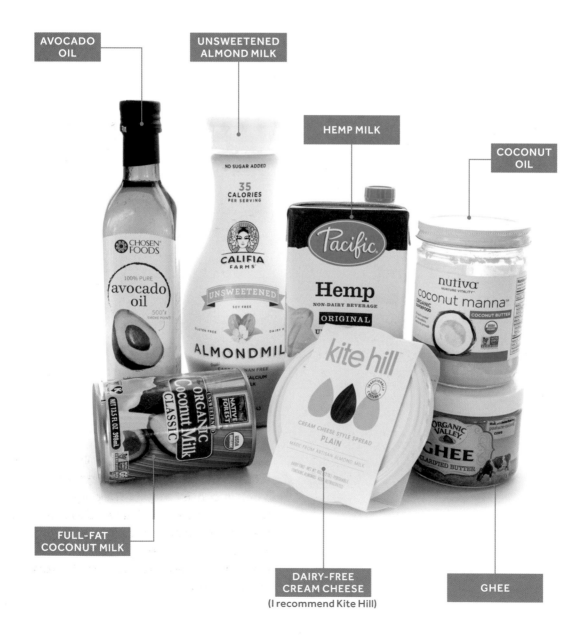

AVOCADO OIL

UNSWEETENED ALMOND MILK

HEMP MILK

COCONUT OIL

FULL-FAT COCONUT MILK

DAIRY-FREE CREAM CHEESE
(I recommend Kite Hill)

GHEE

Specialty Ingredients

While I try very hard to stick with basic and easily sourced ingredients, I also want to give you the best possible keto dessert experience, and that means sometimes using specialty items that are harder to find and may need to be purchased online. But given the increasing popularity of keto diets, I suspect it won't be long before many of these items appear in stores across the country.

Sugar-free chocolate bars and chocolate chips—When I first started creating low-carb recipes, there really was no good sugar-free chocolate on the market. There were Hershey's sugar-free chocolate chips, but they were (and still are) sweetened with maltitol, which spikes blood sugar as much as real sugar. But now there are several great brands, like Lily's, ChocoPerfection, Coco Polo, and Lakanto, among others. Lily's is my go-to for baking, especially since no other brand makes chocolate chips.

I am starting to see Lily's and Coco Polo chocolate in many regular grocery chains, and stores like Whole Foods sell the chips and the dark chocolate baking bars. But I also like to wait for an online sale and stock up.

Grass-fed gelatin and collagen powder—These items are really useful for many keto desserts, giving them a better consistency and helping them hold together. You can also use standard gelatin, such as Knox, but you will need less of it, and you will need to make sure it "blooms" first, which takes an extra step.

Hazelnut meal—This is really just ground hazelnuts, but it's difficult to grind them finely enough at home. It makes for tasty cookies and brownies. Bob's Red Mill hazelnut meal can be found in the gluten-free aisle of some stores.

Peanut flour—In this case, it's not just ground peanuts. The best peanut flour has been partially defatted, which gives it a fine and powdery texture and makes it very absorbent. I like Anthony's brand, which I buy online, but many grocery stores carry "powdered peanut butter," like the PB2 brand, which you can use as well.

Protein powder—Gluten is a protein, and in its absence, another dry powdery protein can help keto baked goods rise and hold together. Protein powder is not used in many recipes in this book, but it is useful, and a little goes a long way. You can use whey protein, egg white protein, or any number of vegan protein powders. Get an unflavored variety if you can. Vanilla-flavored protein powder will work, too, if you leave out any vanilla extract in the recipe.

Cacao butter (aka cocoa butter)—I am surprised that stores are not yet carrying cacao butter, as it's an incredibly useful, delicious, and healthy ingredient. In the recipes in this book, I mostly use it to thin out the chocolate coating for keto candies and bars. But it's great in other desserts, too; it lends a white chocolate flavor and is completely solid at room temperature.

Coconut butter (aka coconut manna)—Coconut butter is made from ground coconut meat and is solid at room temperature. It gives dairy-free keto candies and fudge a great consistency. You can find it in some high-end grocery stores, like Whole Foods, as well as online.

Yacón syrup—Yacón is a sweet-tasting syrup derived from the yacón plant grown in South America. It is said to have a low glycemic index (GI) and a minimal effect on blood sugar levels. I don't trust the glycemic index very much because they used to say the same thing about agave, and agave spiked my blood sugar tremendously. To play it safe, I use very small amounts of yacón syrup (no more than 2 teaspoons) to give certain recipes a brown sugar or caramel flavor or appearance. You could also use blackstrap molasses in these recipes, or you can skip it altogether.

Extracts and flavorings—These little bottles of fun can really transform your dessert creations. Many basic flavors, such as peppermint, almond, and lemon, can be found in the baking aisle of your local grocery store, but others are more easily found online. They aren't expensive, and a small 2-ounce bottle can go a long way. I always have a wide array of natural flavorings in my pantry, everything from cherry to anise and even pineapple (although I haven't used it yet and forgot what I bought it for, but it will make its way into something soon enough). For the recipes in this book, consider getting almond, caramel, coconut, hazelnut, lemon, maple, orange, and peppermint.

Natural food coloring—You absolutely do not need this, but it's kind of fun. You can certainly go *au naturel* with your frostings and fillings, but if you want to amp up the color a bit, there are a few vegetable-based food dyes on the market. I like India Tree and Food Colors From Nature by ColorKitchen. Be forewarned: The yellow powder from ColorKitchen is incredibly vibrant. Don't even think about using the whole envelope!

Xanthan gum—This is useful stuff for thickening puddings and fillings. A very little goes a long way; a bag of it lasts me more than two years. I store it in a jar in my freezer. You can find it in the gluten-free aisle of many grocery stores.

Essential Equipment

Baking sheets—Versatile, multi-purpose, and good for everything from cookies to sheet cakes. Be sure to use rimmed baking sheets for cakes and for anything that might easily slide off the pan.

Glass or ceramic pie pan—A 9-inch pan for pies and tarts.

Square baking pans—For bars, brownies, and cakes. I use a 9-inch square pan, but an 8-inch will do as well. Just remember that your baked goods may take a little longer to cook in the smaller pan since they will be deeper. Look for a pan with sides at least 2 inches deep, and use light-colored pans for more even baking.

Ramekins—4- and 8-ounce ceramic ramekins for individual cakes, custards, and even cookies!

Parchment paper—A low-carb baker's best friend.

Cake pans—A round 8- or 9-inch pan for cakes, with sides at least 2 inches deep. Again, use light-colored pans for more even baking.

Food processor or blender—A good food processor or blender can cut down prep time significantly.

Muffin pans—For candies and cupcakes. I use both standard-size 12-well pans and mini-size 24-well pans.

Electric mixer—A smaller handheld mixer is fine.

Measuring cups and spoons—Accurate measurements are the key to dessert success.

Mixing bowls—It's good to have a few bowls that are heatproof and microwave-safe for melting chocolate.

Whisks, rubber spatulas, and wooden spoons—Mixing and stirring are kind of important here!

Special Equipment

In the spirit of keeping things easy, I tried to steer clear of calling for too much specialty equipment. But if you're looking to up your keto dessert game, here are some gadgets and toys that you might want to invest in.

Kitchen scale—I've provided the measurements of most ingredients in volume (cups and tablespoons), but for flours and meals, I've also provided the approximate weight in grams. Variations between brands of these ingredients can sometimes affect the outcome of your baked goods, and an accurate kitchen scale helps you be more precise.

Silicone baking mats—When you bake as many cookies as I do, you go through a lot of parchment paper. Reusable silicone mats not only keep your cookies from sticking, but protect the bottoms from burning as well.

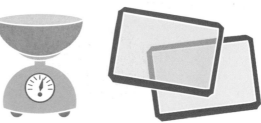

Ice cream maker—You definitely don't need an ice cream maker, and this book contains only one recipe that uses it. But making your own low-carb ice cream is fun, and in the end, that machine will pay for itself!

Silicone molds—Fun shapes for gummies, fat bombs, and other candies! Silicone liners for both standard- and mini-size muffin pans are also very useful and save on parchment paper.

Slow cooker (6 quarts)—Many people don't realize that you can make many wonderful desserts in a slow cooker. One of my all-time favorite keto chocolate cakes is a slow cooker cake. It's insanely moist and delicious.

Ice pop molds—I really want to put these in the "must-have" category because they aren't expensive and they make great keto treats. For the recipes in this book, you will need a set of six 3-ounce molds.

Decorative cake and tart pans—Don't feel you need to limit yourself to square and round cake pans. Although those shapes are the most useful, more decorative options like Bundt pans and fluted tart pans can give your desserts an easy elegance. I love the little 4-inch tart pans for smaller tarts.

Piping bags and decorating tips—I promise, we aren't getting fancy with frosting. But I often use these bags and tips for adding little stars of whipped cream to cakes and pies or for piping mousse into dessert cups. A few disposable bags and some star-shaped tips are all you really need.

DESSERT PRO CHECKLIST

Ready to get started? Here are a few things you can do to ensure the best results when you make any recipe.

☑ **Read the full recipe first.** It can be tempting to jump in and just start whipping up a delectable treat as you go. But reading the full recipe first will actually save you time and help you avoid costly mistakes. Be sure to make note of the prep time, cook time, and inactive time. You don't want to get partway through a recipe you want to eat right away only to discover that it needs to chill for three hours. Also, be sure to factor in any recipe components, such as a crust or topping, that are listed separately as stand-alone recipes. This helps you plan more accurately for the full time it takes to make a recipe, as well as to get all of the necessary ingredients together.

☑ **Preheat the oven when the instructions say to do so.** Most of the time, this is done at the beginning of a recipe so that the oven is up to temperature when the batter or dough is ready to be baked. But some recipes require you to chill your dough first or to make some other part of the dessert ahead of time.

☑ **Let your ingredients soften or come to room temperature when specified.** Although you can hurry these things along a little (see "Time-Saving Tips" on page 29), you really don't want to skip this step. Properly softened and warmed ingredients make for smoother batters and creamier desserts.

☑ **Measure accurately.** Use liquid measuring cups for liquids and dry measuring cups for dry ingredients. Don't pack your dry ingredients unless a recipe specifically states that you should. Use a kitchen scale if you have one. Do everything you can to measure ingredients as accurately as possible. (See "Weigh Your Flours and Nut Meals" on page 11 for a discussion of the importance of weighing these key ingredients.)

☑ **Use fresh, high-quality ingredients.** Fresh eggs will make your batters fluffier and your puddings tastier. Baking powder and baking soda can lose their leavening ability if they've been sitting around too long. And low-quality chocolate has a nasty habit of seizing more easily.

☑ **Use the right-sized pan.** Try to use the size of pan specified in the recipe. If you must, you can use a pan that is close in size, but know that your baking time will change and your results will be somewhat different. Is your pan smaller? Your baking time will be longer and your baked good will be deeper. Is your pan larger? Your baking time will be shorter and your baked good will be shallower. Watch your goodies carefully as they bake, and use visual and tactile cues to determine doneness.

☑ **Grease . . . and grease again.** If the instructions say to grease a pan, be sure to grease it well, getting into every crevice. For cakes, which can be the most prone to sticking, I usually grease the pan with solid butter, working it into every corner, and then I brush the pan with melted coconut oil. For a dairy-free alternative, you could use ghee or solid coconut oil and then melted coconut oil. Or use parchment paper or silicone liners when possible. Keto baked goods can stick a little, so do what you can to minimize breakage and cracking.

☑ **Bake in the middle of the oven.** Unless otherwise specified in a recipe, the middle rack of the oven is the best place for baked goods. This allows heat to circulate evenly around the baked goods. If your oven has a hot spot toward the back, as mine does, consider turning the pan around halfway through baking.

☑ **Don't be a slave to the clock.** Mixing times, baking times, and cooking times are meant to be guidelines, not hard-and-fast rules. Ovens and stovetops vary in temperature, pans vary in weight and color, and some mixers, food processors, and blenders are more powerful than others. Rely more on the visual and tactile cues given in the recipe to know when to move on to the next step.

TIME-SAVING TIPS

You really can't rush most desserts. Even the easiest sweets require a bit of care and a little patience to come out really well. I am possibly the world's most impatient person (ask my husband; he will agree with this wholeheartedly), but I've learned that a dessert that needs three hours to set really does need three hours to set. Too often, I've cut into something early only to have the filling ooze out all over my countertop—not the look I was going for.

That being said, there are a few things you can do to cut corners and make things come together a little faster.

When you're in a hurry . . .

1. Think small and spread out. Individual servings of mousse and pudding are going to set a lot faster than a whole batch kept in one big bowl. Foods baked in individual portions, like small ramekins or muffin pans, bake faster. A sheet cake, which has more surface area exposed to the oven heat, bakes much faster as well. Almost any large dessert can be portioned out into individual servings, assuming you have the right pans or dishes to accommodate them.

2. Warm it up. Did you forget to allow time for your butter or cream cheese to soften or for your eggs to come to room temperature? Yeah, me too. I do this constantly. Not to worry; you can gently soften butter or cream cheese in the microwave—about fifteen seconds on high power is all you need. For eggs, just set them in a bowl of very warm water for ten minutes.

3. Freeze it. Need a dessert to set a little faster? Pop it in the freezer for a bit . . . but don't forget about it. Don't let it actually freeze, because that might change the consistency. But let it chill out for a while, and you can shave an hour or possibly two from the setting time. I find that this works well with cheesecakes in particular. Wait to add any decorative touches until after the dessert has set. Berries and chocolate drizzle don't fare so well in the freezer.

4. Microwave it. That big box sitting on your counter or over your stove is a pretty handy tool when you need to melt butter, chocolate, or anything else quickly. But the heat of a microwave can be intense, so you want to melt things carefully. I always do it in 30-second increments on high power, stirring after each increment until it's smooth. If you don't own a microwave, you can always melt ingredients on the stovetop over low heat. When it comes to chocolate, you should do it double boiler style, using a heatproof bowl set over a pan of barely simmering water. (Do not allow the bottom of the bowl to touch the water.)

5. Go for easy elegance. Skip the fancy decorating techniques. Most desserts don't need it anyway, and you will save yourself a lot of time and stress. People always tell me how beautiful my desserts look, but the truth is that I am a lousy cake and cookie decorator. I have neither the patience nor the inclination to futz around with frosting, although I like my desserts to look pretty and inviting. Consider using these easy decorating techniques:

- Add a dollop of whipped cream or a drizzle of melted chocolate. These things have the added benefit of hiding any mistakes you might have made. I like to say that chocolate ganache fixes everything!

- Use Bundt pans and fun cake or candy molds for instant elegance—no decorating needed.

- Embrace the rustic look. A hundred years ago, cakes were served naked, without piles of sugary frosting slathered all over them. If the cake itself is tasty enough, why bother with the extras?

- In that same vein, a sprinkling of powdered sweetener or cocoa powder can accent a dessert nicely. Or try shaving a little bit of dark chocolate over the top. You can do this to the whole dessert or as you plate individual servings.

- Fresh berries and a sprig of mint add contrast and brightness to any dessert. If it's a citrus-based dessert, add a thin slice of lemon or lime or a little grated zest.

Store-Bought Shortcuts

Sometimes you really just want someone else to make dessert for you. I get that, I really do. However, the keto lifestyle hasn't come quite that far yet, although I do hear tell of keto bakeries and grocery stores popping up in various locations across the country. (Does anyone volunteer to start one in Portland, Oregon? Pretty please???) As a general rule, I say it's still best to make your own desserts at home, where you can control the ingredients and you know exactly what's going into your treats.

A few brands are venturing out into the world of keto baking mixes. On the whole, I don't really find using these mixes that much easier than making desserts from scratch, as you still have to mix them up and bake them. But they can save you a bit of time and a few dishes in a pinch. They can also be great for baking with kids or taking with you when traveling if you will have access to a kitchen.

There are also brands creating prepackaged cookies and brownies, and some of them are pretty decent. Let's be honest: freshly made is always going to taste better than prepackaged, but these desserts can be good in a pinch or on the go.

As always with store-bought products, you need to be a label reader. The ketogenic diet is such a hot-ticket item these days that brands are using the term quite loosely. Just because something calls itself keto-friendly doesn't necessarily mean that it's appropriate for a real keto lifestyle.

Here are my choices for the best convenience desserts and dessert mixes.

BAKING MIXES

Good Dee's—This brand of cookie, brownie, and cake mixes was started by Deana Karim, who follows a low-carb lifestyle herself. She wanted better options than the artificial sweetener–filled mixes on the market, so she created her own, and I think she's done a great job. These get a thumbs-up from my kids!

Swerve—I've been holding this card close to my chest for a while, as I have had the distinct honor of test-driving and photographing Swerve's new line of baking mixes. It includes a vanilla cake mix, a chocolate cake mix, and a chocolate chip cookie mix. They are fantastic—how could I expect any less from the makers of my favorite keto sweetener? The chocolate cake mix is so good that I am sort of jealous I didn't develop it myself. Truth.

PREPACKAGED COOKIES

Keto Kookie—Frankly, this is the only prepackaged cookie that wins my wholehearted approval. Others I have tried are tasteless, or I simply don't trust the ingredients. I have tested Keto Kookies on myself, and they barely raise my blood sugar. They have become my go-to choice of travel snacks.

ICE CREAM AND ICE CREAM BARS

Tread carefully here, my friend. There are a lot of low-sugar ice creams and frozen desserts on the market nowadays. Some contain questionable ingredients (including sugar!), and many really aren't that low-carb. One calls itself keto-friendly, but it's also nonfat, which for me defeats the purpose. If you want to use brands like Halo Top or Enlightened, stick with the plain flavors and consume them sparingly.

But there is a new kid in town, and I am really excited about it. Rebel Creamery is just about to launch, and it is truly a keto ice cream—high-fat, low-carb, no-sugar-added, creamy goodness. I am delighted that someone is finally answering the call for the real deal. Rebel Creamery sent me some of their chocolate ice cream to try, and it tastes very much like my Chocolate Fat Bomb Ice Cream (page 128), so I approve. Watch for them . . . I expect great things!

CHOCOLATE HAZELNUT SPREAD

There are a lot of these spreads on the market, and, as a chocolate hazelnut aficionado, I can say that some are better than others. I think I've tried them all. Though my homemade version (see page 170) is my favorite, I sometimes buy the jarred kind for the convenience factor.

NutiLight—This one is quite good and comes in both dark chocolate and milk chocolate varieties. I much prefer the dark chocolate.

Nougat Crème by KZ Clean Eating—This Swiss brand is my favorite by far. It's incredibly creamy and rich; I like to smear a bit on a piece of low-carb chocolate when I'm in the mood for a quick dessert. But it's also much more expensive than other brands, so I use it very sparingly.

MIX-AND-MATCH DESSERTS

It is my dearest wish that you will not think of the recipes in this book as *faits accomplis*, but as building blocks for creating other wonderful desserts. The mark of a great home cook is the ability to recognize how the various components of a dish might be used to make another entirely different dish. I want this book to be a source of inspiration and a jumping-off point into the sweet side of keto.

Here are a few fun ideas to get you started:

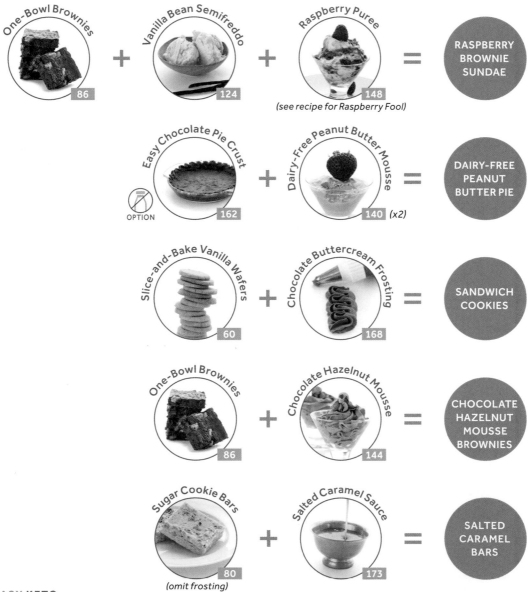

One-Bowl Brownies 86 + Vanilla Bean Semifreddo 124 + Raspberry Puree 148 *(see recipe for Raspberry Fool)* = RASPBERRY BROWNIE SUNDAE

Easy Chocolate Pie Crust 162 OPTION + Dairy-Free Peanut Butter Mousse 140 *(x2)* = DAIRY-FREE PEANUT BUTTER PIE

Slice-and-Bake Vanilla Wafers 60 + Chocolate Buttercream Frosting 168 = SANDWICH COOKIES

One-Bowl Brownies 86 + Chocolate Hazelnut Mousse 144 = CHOCOLATE HAZELNUT MOUSSE BROWNIES

Sugar Cookie Bars 80 *(omit frosting)* + Salted Caramel Sauce 173 = SALTED CARAMEL BARS

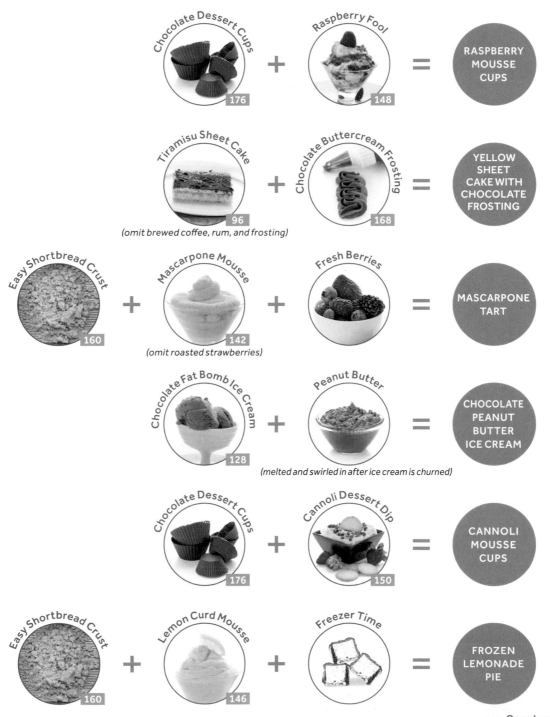

Chocolate Dessert Cups 176 + Raspberry Fool 148 = **RASPBERRY MOUSSE CUPS**

Tiramisu Sheet Cake 96
(omit brewed coffee, rum, and frosting)
+ Chocolate Buttercream Frosting 168 = **YELLOW SHEET CAKE WITH CHOCOLATE FROSTING**

Easy Shortbread Crust 160 + Mascarpone Mousse 142
(omit roasted strawberries)
+ Fresh Berries = **MASCARPONE TART**

Chocolate Fat Bomb Ice Cream 128 + Peanut Butter = **CHOCOLATE PEANUT BUTTER ICE CREAM**
(melted and swirled in after ice cream is churned)

Chocolate Dessert Cups 176 + Cannoli Dessert Dip 150 = **CANNOLI MOUSSE CUPS**

Easy Shortbread Crust 160 + Lemon Curd Mousse 146 + Freezer Time = **FROZEN LEMONADE PIE**

HOW TO USE THE RECIPES

Easy Keto Desserts contains more than fifty low-carb, high-fat dessert recipes and ten "extras"—versatile basics, garnishes, and sauces that will take your healthy desserts to the next level. As is common for cakes, cookies, and bars, many of these recipes serve eight to twelve people, but I have listed storage instructions for any recipe that yields more than six servings. I have also included a number of small-batch recipes that serve four or fewer, because sometimes you need a sweet treat without having a bunch of leftovers hanging around.

Because so many desserts take time to set properly, I have included any inactive time required for each recipe, along with the prep time and cook time.

Quick Reference Icons

Need a big dessert for a party? Want a tasty treat in an instant? Look for these visual cues that tell you a little something extra about each recipe. And be sure to check out the Recipe Quick Reference on pages 184 and 185 to find the easy dessert recipe that fits your needs.

No-Bake—Don't feel like turning on your oven? These no-bake keto desserts are sure to satisfy.

Freezer Friendly—These are desserts that you can make a whole big batch of and then put away for when the cravings strike. Wrap them up tightly to prevent freezer burn!

Small Batch—If it's just you eating keto, or just you and your significant other, you don't always want a lot of sweet treats hanging about. In that case, make one of these recipes that serve four or fewer. I highly recommend the Strawberry Rhubarb Crisp for Two (page 120)!

Feeds a Crowd—Ack! You've been told that you need to bring a dessert to an office party, church potluck, or backyard get-together to share. These desserts serve twelve or more, and they just might win over a few new keto converts.

Almost Instant—All of a sudden, you want a sweet treat, and you want it *now!* All of these desserts are ready in under forty minutes from start to finish. You can whip one up and have it ready in less time than it takes to make and eat your dinner.

I want these recipes to be useful and accessible to as many people as possible, so I have included icons to indicate which recipes are free of common allergens.

 Dairy-Free—More than 50 percent of the recipes in *Easy Keto Desserts* are dairy-free or have a dairy-free option. You will find a lot of great treats here if you are avoiding the creamy white stuff.

 Egg-Free—Making low-carb baked goods without eggs is definitely tricky, but not impossible. Well over 50 percent of the recipes in this book are egg-free as well—mostly the no-bake ones, but a few of the baked goods, too.

 Nut-Free—Nut meals and flours are by far the most useful low-carb flour alternatives, so many of the recipes in this book rely on them. But just under half of these recipes are nut-free. The best replacement for nut flours that I have ever used is sunflower seed flour, so I suggest you look into that if you want to make even more of these recipes nut-free. (I have a recipe for making sunflower seed flour and an accompanying video on my website, *All Day I Dream About Food*.)

Nutritional Information

This cookbook is about enjoying the healthy keto lifestyle to its fullest. To this end, for each recipe I have included key nutritional information per serving: calories, fat, protein, total carbohydrate, and fiber. Please note that erythritol is technically considered a carbohydrate, but it has zero carb impact for most people. It is metabolized and exits the body without ever entering the bloodstream. For the purposes of the keto diet, it should not be counted in the total carbohydrates, although I have included it as a separate line item for anyone who might need that information.

All nutritional information was calculated using MacGourmet, a software program that relies on the USDA National Nutrient Database. I strive to be as accurate as possible, but these numbers are often only estimates based on the average sizes of certain ingredients. I encourage you to calculate your own nutritional information whenever possible.

RECIPES

CHAPTER 1:

CANDY AND CONFECTIONS

PEPPERMINT PATTIES

Yield: 12 patties (1 per serving)
Prep Time: 20 minutes
Cook Time: 5 minutes
Inactive Time: 2 hours

½ cup coconut oil, slightly softened

2 tablespoons coconut cream (from a can of coconut milk; see Tip)

½ cup powdered erythritol-based sweetener

1 teaspoon peppermint extract

3 ounces sugar-free dark chocolate, chopped

½ ounce cacao butter, or 1 tablespoon coconut oil

SWEETENER OPTIONS:
A bulk sweetener is important here because it gives the peppermint mixture some structure. And you want a powdered, or confectioners'-style, sweetener to avoid grittiness.

I used to love York Peppermint Patties—all that bright peppermint flavor enrobed in dark chocolate. Who knew it would be so easy to make your own sugar-free and dairy-free version? Oh, and maybe I should say guilt-free, too.

1. In a medium bowl, beat the coconut oil and coconut cream with an electric mixer until smooth.

2. Add the sweetener and peppermint extract and beat until well combined.

3. Line a baking sheet with wax paper or parchment paper. Dollop a heaping tablespoon of the mixture onto the paper and spread it into a 1½-inch circle. Repeat with the remaining mixture and freeze until firm, about 2 hours.

4. In a heatproof bowl set over a pan of barely simmering water, melt the chocolate and cacao butter together, stirring until smooth. Remove the pan from the heat.

5. Working with one patty at a time and keeping the other patties in the freezer to stay firm, drop a patty into the melted chocolate. Toss to coat well and lift out with a fork, tapping the fork firmly on the edge of the bowl to remove the excess chocolate.

6. Place the patty on a wax paper or parchment paper–lined baking sheet and let set. Repeat with the remaining patties.

STORAGE INSTRUCTIONS: *These peppermint patties will last for up to 2 weeks in the fridge, if you can resist them that long! They can also be stored in the freezer for up to a month, although the color of the chocolate coating may turn a little gray once frozen.*

TIP: *Coconut cream is the thick part of the coconut milk that rises to the top of the can. Simply scoop it out in tablespoons and level it off, taking care to not get any of the thin coconut water underneath. You do not want the coconut cream chilled, as cold cream would be too hard to beat into the coconut oil.*

NUTRITIONAL INFORMATION
CALORIES: 126 | FAT: 13.6g | PROTEIN: 0.4g | CARBS: 2.9g | FIBER: 1.4g | ERYTHRITOL: 11.5g

CHOCOLATE-COVERED CHEESECAKE BITES

Yield: 24 truffles (2 per serving)
Prep Time: 20 minutes
Cook Time: 5 minutes
Inactive Time: 3 to 4 hours

1 (8-ounce) package cream cheese, softened

¼ cup (½ stick) unsalted butter, softened

½ cup powdered erythritol-based sweetener

½ teaspoon vanilla extract

4 ounces sugar-free dark chocolate, chopped

¾ ounce cacao butter, or 1½ tablespoons coconut oil

SWEETENER OPTIONS:
The cheesecake filling can really be sweetened with any sweetener you like.

These easy truffles were a surprise hit with my kids, who usually disdain cheesecake. As an experiment, I put some frozen raspberries in a few of them, and those were even more popular. I highly recommend that little variation!

1. Line a baking sheet with wax paper or parchment paper.

2. In a large bowl, beat the cream cheese and butter with an electric mixer until well combined. Beat in the sweetener and vanilla extract until smooth.

3. Using wet hands, roll the mixture into 1-inch balls and place on the lined baking sheet. Freeze until firm, 3 to 4 hours.

4. In a heatproof bowl set over a pan of barely simmering water, melt the chocolate and cacao butter together, stirring until smooth. Remove the pan from the heat.

5. Working with one ball at a time and keeping the other balls in the freezer to stay firm, drop a ball into the melted chocolate. Toss to coat well and lift out with a fork, tapping the fork firmly on the edge of the bowl to remove the excess chocolate.

6. Place the ball on a wax paper or parchment paper–lined baking sheet and allow to set. Repeat with the remaining cheesecake balls.

7. Drizzle any remaining chocolate decoratively over the coated balls.

STORAGE INSTRUCTIONS: *These truffles are best kept in the fridge, where they will last for up to 5 days. However, they have the best flavor and consistency when served at room temperature, so be sure to let them sit out a bit before eating. They can also be frozen for up to a month, although the chocolate coating may turn a little gray once frozen.*

NUTRITIONAL INFORMATION

CALORIES: 146 | FAT: 13.5g | PROTEIN: 1.6g | CARBS: 4.6g | FIBER: 1.9g | ERYTHRITOL: 12g

VARIATION:
RASPBERRY CHEESECAKE BITES

Follow the directions on the opposite page, but form the cheesecake ball around a frozen raspberry (using 24 raspberries in all). You can do this most easily by flattening the cheesecake ball into a disc and then placing the raspberry in the center and folding the disc around it. Proceed to freeze and then dip in the melted chocolate as directed.

MAPLE WALNUT FUDGE CUPS

Yield: 12 cups (1 per serving)
Prep Time: 5 minutes
Cook Time: 5 minutes
Inactive Time: 1 hour

½ cup (1 stick) salted butter

4 ounces coconut butter

¼ cup powdered erythritol-based sweetener

1 teaspoon yacón syrup (optional, for color and flavor)

2½ teaspoons maple extract

¼ cup chopped toasted walnuts

SWEETENER OPTIONS: These cups do not rely on bulk for consistency, so any sweetener will do.

Fake it 'til you make it, as they say. I don't touch real maple syrup, but a little maple extract allows me to enjoy one of my favorite flavors.

1. Line a mini muffin pan with 12 silicone or parchment paper liners.

2. In a medium saucepan over low heat, melt the butter and coconut butter together, stirring until smooth.

3. Whisk in the sweetener, yacón syrup (if using), and maple extract. Stir in the toasted walnuts.

4. Divide the mixture among the lined mini muffin cups and refrigerate until firm, about 1 hour.

STORAGE INSTRUCTIONS: *These cups need to remain refrigerated for the best consistency and will last for up to 2 weeks. They can also be frozen for up to a month.*

NUTRITIONAL INFORMATION
CALORIES: 150 | FAT: 14.7g | PROTEIN: 1.4g | CARBS: 3.2g | FIBER: 1.9g | ERYTHRITOL: 5g

TOFFEE ALMOND BARK

Yield: 12 servings (about 1 ounce per serving)
Prep Time: 5 minutes
Cook Time: 15 minutes
Inactive Time: 50 minutes

3 tablespoons granulated erythritol-based sweetener

2 tablespoons salted butter

1 cup raw almonds

¼ teaspoon vanilla extract

Pinch of salt

6 ounces sugar-free dark chocolate, chopped

½ ounce cacao butter, or 1 tablespoon coconut oil

SWEETENER OPTIONS:
Sorry, kids, but only granulated erythritol or an erythritol blend will do here. It's impossible to make sugar-free toffee with any other sweetener. Believe me, I've tried!

Coating the almonds with sugar-free toffee takes almond bark to a whole new level. This sweet treat was a huge hit at our New Year's Eve celebration this past year.

1. Line a baking sheet with parchment paper.

2. In a medium saucepan over medium heat, combine the sweetener and butter, stirring until the sweetener dissolves. Add the almonds and bring to a boil. Cook without stirring until the butter darkens to a rich amber color, 5 to 7 minutes.

3. Remove from the heat and stir in the vanilla extract and salt. Spread the almonds in a single layer on the lined baking sheet and let cool for 20 minutes. Break up the almonds with your hands.

4. In a heatproof bowl set over a pan of barely simmering water, melt the chocolate and cacao butter together, stirring until smooth. Add the almonds and toss to coat well. Spread this mixture on the same parchment-lined baking sheet to about 9 inches square.

5. Refrigerate until set, about 30 minutes. Break into pieces with your fingers.

STORAGE INSTRUCTIONS: *This bark is fine on the counter for up to a week. You can also store it in the fridge.*

NUTRITIONAL INFORMATION
CALORIES: 153 | FAT: 13.9g | PROTEIN: 3.3g | CARBS: 8.3g | FIBER: 4.3g | ERYTHRITOL: 6.8g

MACADAMIA COCONUT TRUFFLES

Yield: 24 truffles (2 per serving)
Prep Time: 20 minutes
Cook Time: —
Inactive Time: 1 hour

2 cups roasted unsalted macadamia nuts

⅔ cup plus 3 tablespoons unsweetened shredded coconut, divided

⅓ cup powdered erythritol-based sweetener

2 tablespoons grass-fed collagen powder

1 tablespoon melted coconut oil

1 teaspoon vanilla extract

⅛ teaspoon salt

Macadamia nuts are like Mother Nature's very own fat bombs. These truffles are rich in healthy keto fats and taste like you've been whisked away to a tropical island.

1. Place the macadamia nuts and ⅔ cup of the shredded coconut in a food processor. Process on high until the mixture begins to clump together into a ball.

2. Transfer the nut mixture to a large bowl and stir in the sweetener, collagen, melted coconut oil, vanilla extract, and salt until well combined.

3. Spread the remaining 3 tablespoons of shredded coconut on a shallow plate. Line a baking sheet with wax paper or parchment paper.

4. Working with about 1 tablespoon at a time, squeeze the truffle mixture together in your hands to compact it, then roll it into a ball. Roll each ball in the shredded coconut and place on the lined baking sheet. Refrigerate until firm, about 1 hour.

SWEETENER OPTIONS: You can sweeten these tasty treats however you please!

STORAGE INSTRUCTIONS: *These truffles will keep for about a week in the refrigerator or can be frozen up to a month.*

TIP: *Macadamia nuts are so fatty that they can quickly turn to butter if you process them too long. Be sure to remove the mixture from the food processor when it begins to clump together into one big ball.*

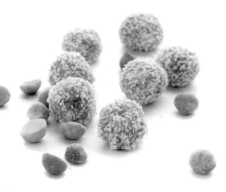

NUTRITIONAL INFORMATION
CALORIES: 202 | FAT: 20.3g | PROTEIN: 2.1g | CARBS: 4.3g | FIBER: 2.5g | ERYTHRITOL: 6.6g

PEANUT BUTTER AND JAM CUPS

Yield: 12 cups (1 per serving)
Prep Time: 5 minutes
Cook Time: 10 minutes
Inactive Time: 45 minutes

¾ cup fresh raspberries

¼ cup water

6 to 8 tablespoons powdered erythritol-based sweetener, divided

1 teaspoon grass-fed gelatin

⅔ cup creamy peanut butter (salted)

⅔ cup coconut oil

SWEETENER OPTIONS:
The peanut butter mixture is best made with a powdered bulk sweetener, but you could probably get away with any sweetener if you really prefer.

I've loved the combination of peanut butter and raspberry jam ever since I was a child. I obviously don't do the sandwich version anymore, but these keto cups allow me to enjoy that salty-sweet flavor and feel a little like a kid again.

1. Line a standard-size muffin pan with 12 silicone or parchment paper liners.

2. In a medium saucepan over medium heat, bring the raspberries and water to a boil, then reduce the heat and simmer for 5 minutes. Mash the berries with a fork.

3. Stir in ¼ cup of the powdered sweetener until combined. Whisk in the gelatin, then let cool while you prepare the peanut butter mixture.

4. In a microwave-safe bowl, combine the peanut butter and coconut oil. Microwave on high power for 30 to 60 seconds, until melted. Whisk in 2 to 4 tablespoons of powdered sweetener, depending on how sweet you like it. I prefer mine less sweet.

5. Spoon about 1 tablespoon of the peanut butter mixture into each cup and set in the freezer to firm up, about 15 minutes.

6. Divide the raspberry mixture among the cups and top with the remaining peanut butter mixture. Refrigerate until firm, about 30 minutes.

STORAGE INSTRUCTIONS: *These cups need to stay refrigerated to be firm enough to eat. They will last for up to a week.*

TIP: *Not a fan of peanut butter? No problem. Swap in your favorite nut or seed butter here.*

NUTRITIONAL INFORMATION
CALORIES: 200 | FAT: 19.4g | PROTEIN: 3.6g | CARBS: 4.4g | FIBER: 1.4g | ERYTHRITOL: 10g

WATERMELON LIME GUMMIES

Yield: About 24 mini muffin–size pieces (4 per serving)
Prep Time: 5 minutes
Cook Time: 5 minutes
Inactive Time: 2 hours

Keto gummy candies are easy enough to make, but I managed to make them even easier by using a flavored sugar-free beverage. This way, you don't have to puree or strain any fruit, and carbs are kept to the bare minimum. You could have so much fun with this recipe and make any number of different flavors. My kids couldn't get enough of these gummies; they were gone in one day!

1¼ cups sugar-free watermelon-flavored beverage (see Tip)

⅓ cup fresh lime juice

3 tablespoons grass-fed gelatin

2 tablespoons powdered erythritol-based sweetener, plus more if desired

Special equipment:

Silicone mini muffin pan or gummy mold (optional)

1. In a medium saucepan, combine the watermelon-flavored beverage and lime juice. Whisk in the gelatin and sweetener and bring to a simmer, stirring until the gelatin dissolves. Add more sweetener to taste.

2. Remove from the heat and spoon into the silicone molds. Refrigerate until firm, about 2 hours. You can also line a square baking pan with parchment paper and pour the mixture into that to chill.

3. To unmold, simply push the gummies out from the bottom of the silicone mold, or lift the parchment out of the baking pan and cut into squares.

SWEETENER OPTIONS: Go wild with whatever sweetener you prefer here. Do note that Bai is already sweetened with erythritol, so you need only add sweetener to taste.

STORAGE INSTRUCTIONS: *These gummies need to be kept in the fridge so they don't melt. They will last for up to a week or two.*

TIP: *There are a number of sugar-free flavored beverages on the market, with a wide range of flavors to choose from. I like the ones that are sweetened with erythritol or stevia or both, like Bai. There are fruit-flavored mixes and drops that you can add to water as well.*

NUTRITIONAL INFORMATION
CALORIES: 17 | FAT: 0g | PROTEIN: 3.1g | CARBS: 1.1g | FIBER: 0.1g | ERYTHRITOL: 6.3g

CHAPTER 2:

COOKIES

SLICE-AND-BAKE VANILLA WAFERS

Yield: About 40 cookies
(2 per serving)
Prep Time: 10 minutes
Cook Time: 15 minutes
Inactive Time: 1 to 2 hours

These shortbread-like cookies are delicious on their own, but part of their charm is how they pair well with other desserts, like Cannoli Dessert Dip (page 150). And because you can keep the cookie logs in the freezer for months, you can cut off a few slices any time you have a hankering for a few crisp, buttery cookies. I actually have a log in my freezer right now!

½ cup (1 stick) unsalted butter, softened

½ cup granulated erythritol-based sweetener

1¾ cups (175g) blanched almond flour

2 tablespoons coconut flour

½ teaspoon vanilla extract

¼ teaspoon salt

SWEETENER OPTIONS:
This recipe really relies on a bulk granulated sweetener to achieve the right consistency.

1. In a large bowl, beat the butter and sweetener with an electric mixer until lightened and fluffy, about 2 minutes. Beat in the almond flour, coconut flour, vanilla extract, and salt until well combined.

2. Divide the dough evenly between 2 sheets of wax paper or parchment paper and roll each portion into a log about 1½ inches in diameter. Wrap tightly in the paper and freeze for 1 to 2 hours.

3. Preheat the oven to 325°F and line 2 baking sheets with parchment paper or silicone baking mats. Using a sharp knife, slice the dough crosswise into ¼-inch slices. Place on the lined baking sheets, leaving about 1 inch between wafers.

4. Bake for 5 minutes, then remove from the oven and use a flat-bottomed glass to flatten the cookies slightly. Bake for another 8 to 10 minutes, until the edges are just golden. Remove from the oven and let cool on the pans. The cookies will still be quite soft when they come out of the oven but will firm up as they cool.

SERVING SUGGESTION: *Try using these cookies to sandwich a little of the Chocolate Buttercream Frosting (page 168). Divine!*

STORAGE INSTRUCTIONS: *You can keep the unbaked logs of dough in the freezer for 2 to 3 months. The baked cookies are best stored on the counter for up to 5 days.*

TIP: *Once the dough has been in the freezer for more than 2 hours, it can freeze very hard. Set it out on the counter to soften just long enough that you can slice it without shattering it. Fifteen minutes ought to do.*

NUTRITIONAL INFORMATION
CALORIES: 101 | FAT: 9.3g | PROTEIN: 2.2g | CARBS: 2.5g | FIBER: 1.3g | ERYTHRITOL: 6g

AMARETTI

Yield: About 20 cookies
(2 per serving)
Prep Time: 15 minutes
Cook Time: 22 minutes

2 cups (165g) sliced almonds, plus extra for garnish if desired

½ cup granulated erythritol-based sweetener

¼ cup powdered erythritol-based sweetener, plus extra for dusting if desired

4 large egg whites

½ teaspoon almond extract

Pinch of salt

SWEETENER OPTIONS:
You really have to use a bulk sweetener here. You can do all granulated and skip the powdered version as long as you make sure to grind it well with the sliced almonds, but this mix of the two sweeteners gives the cookies the best consistency.

Amaretti are classic Italian almond cookies made with almond meal and egg whites. They are slightly crispy and slightly chewy, and perfect with an espresso. This recipe is a great way to use up leftover egg whites after making a keto custard or pudding.

1. Preheat the oven to 300°F and line 2 baking sheets with parchment paper. Lightly grease the parchment.

2. In a food processor, process the sliced almonds, granulated sweetener, and powdered sweetener until the mixture resembles coarse crumbs.

3. In a large bowl, use an electric mixer to beat the egg whites with the almond extract and salt until they hold soft peaks. Carefully fold the almond mixture into the egg whites until just combined.

4. Use a cookie scoop or tablespoon to drop the mixture onto the prepared baking sheets, leaving about 1 inch between them. If desired, gently press an almond slice on top of each cookie. Bake for 22 minutes, until just brown around the edges. They will feel like jelly when poked but will firm up as they cool.

5. Remove from the oven and let cool completely on the baking sheets. When cool, gently peel the cookies off the parchment. If desired, dust each cookie with powdered sweetener.

STORAGE INSTRUCTIONS: *These cookies are best kept on the counter for up to 5 days.*

TIP: *I opted for sliced almonds that still had some skin on them for a more rustic look, but you could use blanched almond flour for a finer consistency. Just be sure to weigh the almond flour so that it matches the exact weight I've given here. Otherwise, your cookies will be too dense and heavy.*

NUTRITIONAL INFORMATION

CALORIES: 117 | FAT: 8.8g | PROTEIN: 5.3g | CARBS: 4.1g | FIBER: 2.3g | ERYTHRITOL: 18g

PEANUT BUTTER COOKIES FOR TWO

OPTION

Yield: 2 cookies (1 per serving)
Prep Time: 5 minutes
Cook Time: 12 minutes

1½ tablespoons creamy peanut butter (salted)

1 tablespoon unsalted butter, softened

2 tablespoons granulated erythritol-based sweetener

2 teaspoons lightly beaten egg (see Tip)

¼ teaspoon vanilla extract

2 tablespoons defatted peanut flour

⅛ teaspoon baking powder

Pinch of salt

2 teaspoons sugar-free chocolate chips

If you are like me, you have little self-control around freshly baked peanut butter cookies, especially ones with chocolate chips, like these. This small-batch version solves that problem!

1. Preheat the oven to 325°F and line a baking sheet with parchment paper or a silicone baking mat.

2. In a small bowl, beat the peanut butter, butter, and sweetener with an electric mixer until well combined. Beat in the egg and vanilla extract.

3. Add the peanut flour, baking powder, and salt and mix until the dough comes together. Divide the dough in half and roll each half into a ball.

4. Place the dough balls on the lined baking sheet and press each ball into a disc about ½ inch thick. Top each disc with 1 teaspoon of chocolate chips, pressing them into the dough to adhere.

5. Bake for 10 to 12 minutes, until puffed and just barely golden brown. Remove from the oven and let cool on the pan. The cookies will still be very soft when they come out of the oven but will firm up as they cool.

SWEETENER OPTIONS: A bulk sweetener will give these cookies a better consistency, but you might be able to get away with a non-bulk sweetener here.

DAIRY-FREE OPTION: *Substitute softened coconut oil for the butter.*

TIP: *To measure out 2 teaspoons of egg, simply beat the egg lightly in a bowl first. This breaks up the proteins and combines the egg white with the yolk. You can save the rest of the egg for your breakfast. This recipe also works well with carton egg whites, if you prefer.*

NUTRITIONAL INFORMATION

CALORIES: 163 | FAT: 13.2g | PROTEIN: 4.9g | CARBS: 5.7g | FIBER: 1.9g | ERYTHRITOL: 16g

CREAM CHEESE COOKIES

Yield: About 24 cookies
(2 per serving)
Prep Time: 15 minutes
Cook Time: 12 minutes

4 ounces cream cheese
(½ cup), softened

¼ cup (½ stick) unsalted
butter, softened

½ cup granulated erythritol-
based sweetener

1 large egg, room temperature

½ teaspoon vanilla extract

1½ cups (150g) blanched
almond flour

1 teaspoon baking powder

¼ teaspoon salt

Powdered erythritol-based
sweetener, for dusting

Cream cheese makes for unbelievably tender cookies. These are puffy and soft and almost somewhere between cookie and cake. They need nothing more than a sprinkle of powdered sweetener for garnish.

1. Preheat the oven to 350°F and line a baking sheet with parchment paper or a silicone baking mat.

2. In a large bowl, beat the cream cheese and butter with an electric mixer until smooth. Add the sweetener and continue to beat until well incorporated. Beat in the egg and vanilla extract.

3. Whisk together the almond flour, baking powder, and salt in a medium bowl, then add the flour mixture to the cream cheese mixture and stir until just combined.

4. Drop the dough by rounded tablespoons onto the lined baking sheet; the batter will be quite sticky. Press the cookies down lightly with the heel of your hand to flatten them slightly.

5. Bake for 10 to 12 minutes, until puffed. The cookies will still be very soft and light in color. Remove from the oven and let cool completely on the pan. When cool, dust with powdered sweetener.

SWEETENER OPTIONS:
A bulk sweetener helps give these cookies structure. They may not fare so well with a non-bulk sweetener.

STORAGE INSTRUCTIONS: *These cookies can be stored on the counter for up to 4 days or in the fridge for up to a week. They can also be frozen for up to a month.*

NUTRITIONAL INFORMATION
CALORIES: 154 | FAT: 13.7g | PROTEIN: 4.1g | CARBS: 3.4g | FIBER: 1.5g | ERYTHRITOL: 10g

CHEWY DOUBLE CHOCOLATE COOKIES

OPTION

Yield: About 20 cookies
(2 per serving)
Prep Time: 15 minutes
Cook Time: 12 minutes

These cookies owe their chewiness to the addition of grass-fed gelatin. Weird but true, and it really works!

¾ cup plus 2 tablespoons (88g) blanched almond flour

3 tablespoons cocoa powder

1 tablespoon grass-fed gelatin

½ teaspoon baking soda

½ teaspoon salt

¼ cup (½ stick) unsalted butter, softened

¼ cup creamy almond butter (unsalted)

½ cup granulated erythritol-based sweetener

1 large egg, room temperature

½ teaspoon vanilla extract

⅓ cup sugar-free chocolate chips

1. Preheat the oven to 350°F and line 2 baking sheets with parchment paper or silicone baking mats.

2. In a medium bowl, whisk together the almond flour, cocoa powder, gelatin, baking soda, and salt.

3. In a large bowl, beat the butter, almond butter, and sweetener with an electric mixer until well combined. Beat in the egg and vanilla extract, then beat in the almond flour mixture until the dough comes together. Stir in the chocolate chips.

4. Roll the dough into 1-inch balls and place a few inches apart on the lined baking sheets. Use the heel of your hand to press the cookies down to about ½ inch thick.

5. Bake for 12 minutes, until the cookies have spread and puffed up a bit. They will still be very soft to the touch. Remove from the oven and let cool completely on the pan.

SWEETENER OPTIONS: These cookies are best made with a bulk sweetener.

DAIRY-FREE OPTION: *Use coconut oil in place of the butter.*

STORAGE INSTRUCTIONS: *The cookies are fine on the counter for up to 5 days or can be kept in the fridge for up to a week. The best way to freeze them is unbaked. Simply roll the balls, lay them out on a parchment-lined baking sheet, and freeze. Once they are solid, you can pop them into a bag or a container, and they will keep for up to 2 months. To bake from frozen, simply let them thaw on a baking sheet.*

NUTRITIONAL INFORMATION

CALORIES: 180 | FAT: 15.1g | PROTEIN: 5.5g | CARBS: 6.9g | FIBER: 3.4g | ERYTHRITOL: 12g

NO-BAKE PEANUT BUTTER CARAMEL COOKIES

Yield: 16 cookies (1 per serving)
Prep Time: 5 minutes (not including time to make caramel sauce)
Cook Time: 10 minutes
Inactive Time: 1 hour

Peanut butter and caramel are a match made in dessert heaven—especially when they come together in an easy-to-make no-bake cookie.

1 recipe Caramel Sauce (page 172)

¾ cup creamy peanut butter (salted)

½ teaspoon caramel or vanilla extract

¾ cup unsweetened flaked coconut

¾ cup sliced almonds

3 ounces pork rinds, finely crushed (about 1⅓ cups)

¼ cup powdered erythritol-based sweetener

1. Line a baking sheet with wax paper or parchment paper.

2. In a saucepan over low heat, stir the caramel sauce and peanut butter until melted and smooth. Stir in the extract and remove from the heat.

3. In a food processor, pulse the flaked coconut and sliced almonds together until the mixture resembles oatmeal.

4. Add the coconut and almond mixture, crushed pork rinds, and sweetener to the caramel mixture and stir to combine well.

5. Drop the mixture by rounded tablespoons onto the lined baking sheet, leaving about 2 inches between them. Press the cookies with the palm of your hand to flatten them.

6. Refrigerate for about 1 hour to firm up.

SWEETENER OPTIONS: A powdered bulk sweetener works best here.

STORAGE INSTRUCTIONS: *These soft cookies are best kept in the fridge. They will last for up to a week.*

TIP: *Does it seem odd to put pork rinds in a dessert? Well, it works! It gives the cookies a little crunch as well as cuts down on carbs.*

NUTRITIONAL INFORMATION

CALORIES: 200 | FAT: 16.6g | PROTEIN: 7.3g | CARBS: 5.1g | FIBER: 1.7g | ERYTHRITOL: 9.4g

CHOCOLATE HAZELNUT THUMBPRINTS

OPTION

Yield: 24 cookies (2 per serving)

Prep Time: 15 minutes (not including time to make chocolate hazelnut spread)

Cook Time: 18 minutes

2 cups (200g) hazelnut meal

½ cup granulated erythritol-based sweetener

½ teaspoon baking powder

¼ teaspoon salt

1 large egg

¼ cup (½ stick) unsalted butter, melted but not hot

½ teaspoon vanilla extract

½ cup Homemade Chocolate Hazelnut Spread (page 170)

SWEETENER OPTIONS: These cookies can be sweetened with any sweetener you prefer.

Hi, my name is Carolyn, and I am obsessed with chocolate and hazelnut.

1. Preheat the oven to 325°F and line a baking sheet with parchment paper or a silicone baking mat.

2. In a medium bowl, whisk together the hazelnut meal, sweetener, baking powder, and salt. Stir in the egg, melted butter, and vanilla extract until the dough comes together.

3. Roll the dough into 1-inch balls and place a few inches apart on the lined baking sheet. Press the balls down with the palm of your hand to about ½ inch thick. Use your thumb to make a well in the center of each cookie.

4. Bake for 15 to 18 minutes, until golden brown around the edges and just firm to the touch. Remove from the oven and let cool completely on the pan.

5. Once cool, dab about 1 teaspoon of the chocolate hazelnut spread into each well.

DAIRY-FREE OPTION: *Use coconut oil in place of the butter.*

STORAGE INSTRUCTIONS: *These cookies are best stored in the fridge, as the filling can be pretty goopy otherwise. But I like the flavors best at room temperature, so I always let them sit out for 15 minutes or so before eating them.*

NUTRITIONAL INFORMATION

CALORIES: 220 | FAT: 20.1g | PROTEIN: 4.3g | CARBS: 4.9g | FIBER: 2.9g | ERYTHRITOL: 12.5g

DEEP-DISH CHOCOLATE CHIP COOKIES

OPTION

Yield: 2 cookies (1 per serving)
Prep Time: 5 minutes
Cook Time: 20 minutes

3 tablespoons unsalted butter

3 tablespoons powdered erythritol-based sweetener

1 tablespoon lightly beaten egg (see Tip, page 64)

⅛ teaspoon vanilla extract

¼ cup (25g) blanched almond flour

¼ teaspoon baking soda

1 tablespoon sugar-free chocolate chips

SWEETENER OPTIONS:
A bulk sweetener will give these cookies the best consistency, but you could really use almost anything here.

Gooey chocolate chip cookies warm from the oven—is there anything better?

1. Preheat the oven to 325°F and grease two 4-ounce ramekins or cute little 3½-inch cast-iron skillets, if you can find them!

2. In a microwave-safe bowl, microwave the butter on high until melted, about 30 seconds. Stir in the sweetener until dissolved, then stir in the beaten egg and vanilla extract.

3. Add the almond flour and baking soda and stir until well combined. Divide the dough between the greased ramekins and press to the edges. Divide the chocolate chips between the ramekins and press gently into the dough.

4. Bake for 15 to 20 minutes, until golden brown but still soft to the touch. The baking time will depend somewhat on how deep your ramekins are.

5. Remove from the oven and let cool in the ramekins for a few minutes before serving. Eat directly from the ramekin with a spoon.

DAIRY-FREE OPTION: *Use coconut oil in place of the butter.*

SERVING SUGGESTION: *These cookies are absolutely dreamy with some Vanilla Bean Semifreddo (page 124), traditional Whipped Cream (page 164), or Coconut Whipped Cream (page 166).*

TIP: *If you only have bigger ramekins, you can bake both servings in one 8-ounce ramekin. The baking time will increase.*

NUTRITIONAL INFORMATION

CALORIES: 275 | FAT: 25.7g | PROTEIN: 4.6g | CARBS: 5.6g | FIBER: 2.5g | ERYTHRITOL: 22.5g

CHAPTER 3:

BARS

NO-BAKE CHOCOLATE "OATMEAL" BARS

Yield: 16 bars (1 per serving)
Prep Time: 15 minutes
Cook Time: 10 minutes
Inactive Time: 1 hour

I used to love the oatmeal fudge bars from Starbucks. With these rich, oatmeal-like bars, I don't miss them any longer. Grinding up flaked coconut and sliced almonds makes a great oatmeal substitute.

CRUST:

1 cup unsweetened flaked coconut

1 cup sliced almonds

½ cup (1 stick) unsalted butter

½ cup granulated erythritol-based sweetener

1 teaspoon yacón syrup (optional)

½ teaspoon vanilla extract

1 cup (100g) blanched almond flour

¼ teaspoon salt

FILLING:

1¼ cups heavy whipping cream

4 ounces unsweetened chocolate, finely chopped

2 tablespoons unsalted butter

½ cup powdered erythritol-based sweetener

½ teaspoon vanilla extract

SWEETENER OPTIONS:
Both the crust and the filling really need a bulk sweetener for consistency. The sweetener for the filling should be a powdered version to avoid grittiness.

TO MAKE THE CRUST:

1. Line a 9-inch square baking pan with parchment paper, leaving an overhang for easy removal.

2. In a food processor, process the coconut and sliced almonds until they resemble grains of oatmeal. Set aside.

3. In a medium saucepan over medium heat, bring the butter, sweetener, yacón syrup (if using), and vanilla extract to a low boil, whisking to combine well. Remove from the heat.

4. Add the ground coconut and almonds, almond flour, and salt. Stir until well combined. Press about two-thirds of the mixture into the bottom of the lined baking pan.

TO MAKE THE FILLING AND ASSEMBLE:

5. In a medium saucepan over medium heat, bring the cream just to a simmer. Remove from the heat and add the chopped chocolate and butter. Let sit for 4 minutes to melt.

6. Add the sweetener and vanilla extract and whisk until well combined and smooth.

7. Pour the filling over the crust in the pan. Sprinkle with the remaining crust mixture and refrigerate until firm, about 1 hour.

8. Lift out by the overhanging parchment and cut into 16 bars.

STORAGE INSTRUCTIONS: *These bars will keep in the fridge for up to a week, but they are best served at room temperature. They can be wrapped up tightly and frozen for up to a month.*

NUTRITIONAL INFORMATION
CALORIES: 275 | FAT: 25.5g | PROTEIN: 4.4g | CARBS: 6.5g | FIBER: 3.2g | ERYTHRITOL: 15g

SUGAR COOKIE BARS

Yield: 16 bars (1 per serving)
Prep Time: 15 minutes (not including time to make sprinkles)
Cook Time: 18 minutes

No dessert cookbook would be complete without a sugar cookie recipe. Pressing the dough into a pan allows you to skip the time-consuming task of rolling and cutting the cookies individually, and you still get the same great flavor.

BARS:

2 cups (200g) blanched almond flour

2 tablespoons coconut flour

½ cup granulated erythritol-based sweetener

½ teaspoon baking powder

¼ teaspoon salt

½ cup (1 stick) unsalted butter, melted but not hot

1 large egg

½ teaspoon vanilla extract

VANILLA FROSTING:

½ cup (1 stick) unsalted butter, softened

2 ounces cream cheese (¼ cup), softened

½ cup powdered erythritol-based sweetener

2 to 4 tablespoons heavy whipping cream, room temperature

½ teaspoon vanilla extract

Natural red food coloring (optional)

1 tablespoon Coconut Sprinkles (page 175)

TO MAKE THE BARS:

1. Preheat the oven to 325°F and grease a 9-inch square baking pan.

2. In a large bowl, whisk together the almond flour, coconut flour, granulated sweetener, baking powder, and salt. Stir in the butter, egg, and vanilla extract until well combined.

3. Spread the dough evenly in the greased baking pan and bake until the edges are golden brown, about 18 minutes. The center will still be very soft. Remove from the oven and let cool completely in the pan.

TO MAKE THE FROSTING AND ASSEMBLE:

4. In a medium bowl, beat the butter and cream cheese with an electric mixer until smooth. Beat in the powdered sweetener.

5. Add the heavy cream 1 tablespoon at a time until the frosting is spreadable. Beat in the vanilla extract and a small amount of food coloring, if using, until well combined.

6. Spread the frosting evenly over the cooled cookie and sprinkle with coconut sprinkles. Cut into 16 bars.

STORAGE INSTRUCTIONS: *These bars should be kept refrigerated and will last for up to 5 days. They are best served at room temperature.*

SWEETENER OPTIONS:
A bulk sweetener gives both the bars and the frosting the best consistency, but you can get away with a non-bulk sweetener as well.

NUTRITIONAL INFORMATION
CALORIES: 218 | FAT: 20.5g | PROTEIN: 3.9g | CARBS: 3.9g | FIBER: 1.8g | ERYTHRITOL: 15g

DAIRY-FREE PEANUT BUTTER BARS

Yield: 16 bars (1 per serving)
Prep Time: 15 minutes
Cook Time: 5 minutes
Inactive Time: 1 hour

BARS:

¾ cup creamy peanut butter (salted)

½ cup plus 2 tablespoons coconut oil

⅔ cup powdered erythritol-based sweetener

1 teaspoon vanilla extract

2 cups (200g) defatted peanut flour (see Tip)

CHOCOLATE GLAZE:

3 ounces sugar-free dark chocolate, chopped

1 tablespoon coconut oil

> **SWEETENER OPTIONS:** These delicious bars don't require a bulk sweetener, but they may need a little more peanut flour to firm up properly if you use a non-bulk sweetener.

Around these parts, my peanut butter bars are practically famous. My friends and neighbors make them frequently. I took this dairy-free version to CrossFit and nary a crumb was left.

TO MAKE THE BARS:

1. Line a 9-inch square baking pan with parchment paper, leaving an overhang for easy removal.

2. Place the peanut butter and coconut oil in a large microwave-safe bowl. Microwave on high power until melted, then whisk until smooth. Alternatively, you can melt them together in a saucepan over low heat. Stir in the sweetener and vanilla extract until well combined.

3. Stir in the peanut flour until the dough comes together. It should be a stiff dough that you can pick up with your hands. If it's too soft, add more peanut flour, 1 tablespoon at a time, until it firms up.

4. Press the dough firmly and evenly into the lined baking pan. Cover with a sheet of wax paper or parchment paper and use a flat-bottomed glass or measuring cup to press and smooth the top.

TO MAKE THE GLAZE AND ASSEMBLE:

5. Place the chocolate and coconut oil in a microwave-safe bowl. Microwave on high power in 30-second increments, stirring after each increment, until melted and smooth. You can also set the bowl over a pan of barely simmering water and stir the chocolate mixture until melted.

6. Pour the glaze over the bars and use a knife or an offset spatula to spread it to the edges. Refrigerate for 1 hour, until the chocolate is set.

7. Lift out by the overhanging parchment and cut into 16 bars.

NUTRITIONAL INFORMATION
CALORIES: 211 | FAT: 19g | PROTEIN: 5.5g | CARBS: 7.2g | FIBER: 2.9g | ERYTHRITOL: 11g

STORAGE INSTRUCTIONS: *These bars are best kept in the refrigerator and will last for at least a week.*

TIP: *Do not pack the peanut flour as you measure it out. It's very fine and powdery, so packing it can make a huge difference in the outcome of the bars. Simply scoop and level, as you would with any flour.*

NO-BAKE BLUEBERRY CHEESECAKE BARS

Yield: 16 bars (1 per serving)
Prep Time: 15 minutes (not including time to make crust)
Cook Time: 7 minutes
Inactive Time: 2 hours

The creamy richness of cheesecake pairs so delightfully with the tangy sweetness of blueberries. If you're a cheesecake fan, these bars are sure to please.

BARS:

1 recipe Easy Shortbread Crust (page 160)

2 (8-ounce) packages cream cheese, softened

½ cup powdered erythritol-based sweetener

1 teaspoon grated lemon zest

¼ cup heavy whipping cream, room temperature

BLUEBERRY TOPPING:

1 cup frozen blueberries

¼ cup water

¼ cup powdered erythritol-based sweetener

1 tablespoon fresh lemon juice

¼ teaspoon xanthan gum

Fresh mint, for garnish (optional)

SWEETENER OPTIONS:
Go ahead and use any sweetener you like, except for granulated bulk sweeteners. Because these bars are not baked, a granulated sweetener would be too gritty.

TO MAKE THE BARS:

1. Press the shortbread crust mixture firmly and evenly into the bottom of a 9-inch square baking pan. Freeze the crust while you prepare the cheesecake filling. (Freezing the crust will help it hold together when you spread the filling on top.)

2. In a large bowl, use an electric mixer to beat the cream cheese with the sweetener and lemon zest until smooth. Beat in the cream until well combined.

3. Spread the filling over the crust. Refrigerate until firm, at least 2 hours.

TO MAKE THE TOPPING AND ASSEMBLE:

4. In a medium saucepan over medium heat, bring the blueberries, water, and sweetener to a boil, then simmer for 5 minutes.

5. Remove from the heat and stir in the lemon juice. Sprinkle with the xanthan gum and whisk quickly to combine. Let cool before using.

6. Pour the blueberry topping over the cheesecake—either the entire pan or individual servings. Garnish with fresh mint, if desired.

STORAGE INSTRUCTIONS: *As with any cheesecake dessert, these bars need to be kept in the fridge and will last for up to 5 days.*

NUTRITIONAL INFORMATION
CALORIES: 193 | FAT: 16.7g | PROTEIN: 3.7g | CARBS: 4.5g | FIBER: 1.2g | ERYTHRITOL: 16g

ONE-BOWL BROWNIES

Yield: 16 brownies (1 per serving)
Prep Time: 10 minutes
Cook Time: 20 minutes

¾ cup avocado oil

¾ cup granulated erythritol-based sweetener

3 large eggs

½ teaspoon vanilla extract

½ cup (50g) blanched almond flour

⅓ cup cocoa powder

½ teaspoon baking powder

¼ teaspoon salt

½ cup chopped raw walnuts or pecans (optional)

SWEETENER OPTIONS: A bulk sweetener is important to give these a true brownie texture.

This easy, dairy-free recipe results in fudgy goodness. Try these brownies with a little Coconut Whipped Cream (page 166) on top for sheer keto decadence!

1. Preheat the oven to 325°F and grease a 9-inch square baking pan.

2. In a large bowl, whisk together the oil, sweetener, eggs, and vanilla extract.

3. Add the almond flour, cocoa powder, baking powder, and salt and whisk until well combined. Stir in the chopped nuts, if using.

4. Bake for 20 minutes, or until the edges are set but the center is still a little soft to the touch. Bake longer if you prefer cakier brownies.

5. Remove from the oven and let cool completely in the pan. Then cut into 16 squares.

SERVING SUGGESTION: *If you don't need to be dairy-free, these brownies would be dreamy topped with Chocolate Buttercream Frosting (page 168) or a scoop of Vanilla Bean Semifreddo (page 124).*

STORAGE INSTRUCTIONS: *Because of their moisture content, these brownies are best kept in the fridge for up to 5 days. I like to let them come to room temperature before eating.*

NUTRITIONAL INFORMATION

CALORIES: 113 | FAT: 15.5g | PROTEIN: 3.2g | CARBS: 2.3g | FIBER: 1.3g | ERYTHRITOL: 11.3g

DAIRY-FREE COCONUT BARS

Yield: 16 bars (1 per serving)
Prep Time: 10 minutes
Cook Time: 5 minutes
Inactive Time: 1 hour 10 minutes

The other day, my next-door neighbor came charging out of his house calling my name. I thought I was in trouble! He accosted me simply so he could rave about the coconut bars I'd left on his doorstep. I think they taste a lot like Mounds bars. One of my recipe testers suggested adding a few almonds to the top for an Almond Joy–like version. I say that part is up to you!

2 cups unsweetened shredded coconut

½ cup powdered erythritol-based sweetener

3 tablespoons grass-fed collagen powder

½ cup plus 1 tablespoon coconut oil, softened, divided

¼ cup full-fat coconut milk

½ teaspoon coconut extract

3 ounces sugar-free dark chocolate, chopped

1. Line a 9-inch square baking pan with parchment paper, leaving an overhang for easy removal.

2. In a medium bowl, whisk together the coconut, sweetener, and collagen. Add ½ cup of the coconut oil, the coconut milk, and coconut extract. Stir until well combined.

3. Press the coconut mixture firmly and evenly into the bottom of the lined baking pan and refrigerate until firm, about 1 hour.

4. In a heatproof bowl set over a pan of barely simmering water, stir the chopped chocolate and remaining tablespoon of coconut oil until melted and smooth. Spread the melted chocolate mixture over the chilled coconut base and allow to set, about 10 minutes.

5. Lift out by the overhanging parchment and cut into 16 bars.

SWEETENER OPTIONS: These bars rely on a powdered bulk sweetener for the right consistency.

STORAGE INSTRUCTIONS: *Because there is no dairy in these bars, they can stay out on the counter for a few days, but they do get mighty soft that way. In the fridge, they can last for over a week. I prefer the flavor at room temperature, but they are good either way.*

NUTRITIONAL INFORMATION
CALORIES: 173 | FAT: 17.2g | PROTEIN: 3.3g | CARBS: 4.9g | FIBER: 2.4g | ERYTHRITOL: 8.6g

NO-BAKE FRENCH SILK PIE BARS

Yield: 16 bars (1 per serving)
Prep Time: 30 minutes (not including time to make crust or whipped cream)
Cook Time: 5 minutes
Inactive Time: 2 hours 10 minutes

Although these silky-rich chocolate bars are a little heavier on the prep time than most recipes in this book, they require no baking and are worth every second!

BARS:

1 recipe Easy Shortbread Crust (page 160)

3 ounces unsweetened chocolate, chopped

¾ cup (1½ sticks) unsalted butter, softened

⅔ cup powdered erythritol-based sweetener

1 teaspoon vanilla extract

½ teaspoon espresso powder (optional)

¼ teaspoon salt

3 large eggs

GARNISH:

¾ recipe Whipped Cream (page 164)

½ ounce sugar-free dark chocolate

SWEETENER OPTIONS:
You could probably get away with almost any sweetener you prefer in the filling.

TO MAKE THE BARS:

1. Press the shortbread crust mixture firmly and evenly into the bottom of a 9-inch square baking pan. Refrigerate the crust while you prepare the filling.

2. In a heatproof bowl set over a pan of barely simmering water, melt the chocolate, stirring until smooth. Alternatively, you can melt the chocolate in a microwave-safe bowl in 30-second increments, stirring after each increment. Remove the bowl from the pan and let cool for 10 minutes.

3. In a large bowl, beat the butter and sweetener with an electric mixer until well combined and fluffy, about 2 minutes. With the mixer running, slowly add the melted chocolate, beating until smooth. Add the vanilla extract, espresso powder (if using), and salt.

4. Add the eggs, one at a time, beating for 5 minutes after each addition. Pour the filling over the chilled crust and smooth the top. Refrigerate until firm, at least 2 hours.

TO GARNISH THE BARS:

5. Spread the whipped cream over the entire chilled dessert or pipe onto individual bars. Grate the chocolate over the top.

NUTRITIONAL INFORMATION
CALORIES: 255 | FAT: 23.7g | PROTEIN: 4.6g | CARBS: 4.6g | FIBER: 2.2g | ERYTHRITOL: 15g

STORAGE INSTRUCTIONS: *These bars must be kept chilled. Because they are made with raw eggs, they should be consumed within 3 days.*

TIPS: *If you are concerned about consuming raw eggs, feel free to use pasteurized eggs, such as Safest Choice brand.*

If you want to cut these into perfect squares with straight edges, make sure to heat up a nice sharp knife first. I hold mine over the flame of my gas stove, but you could run it under boiling water as well.

CHAPTER 4:

CAKES

MINI NO-BAKE
LEMON CHEESECAKES

Yield: 6 mini cheesecakes
(1 per serving)
Prep Time: 20 minutes
Cook Time: —
Inactive Time: 2 hours

Placing individual servings of cheesecake in cupcake liners makes them easy to bake, easy to serve, and easy to clean up!

CRUST:

½ cup blanched almond flour

2 tablespoons powdered erythritol-based sweetener

⅛ teaspoon salt

2 tablespoons unsalted butter, melted

FILLING:

6 ounces cream cheese (¾ cup), softened

¼ cup plus 1 tablespoon powdered erythritol-based sweetener

¼ cup heavy whipping cream, room temperature

2 teaspoons grated lemon zest

2 tablespoons fresh lemon juice

½ teaspoon lemon extract

Natural yellow food coloring (optional)

> **SWEETENER OPTIONS:**
> A powdered bulk sweetener is your best bet for this recipe.

TO MAKE THE CRUST:

1. Line a standard-size muffin pan with 6 silicone or parchment paper liners.

2. In a medium bowl, whisk together the almond flour, sweetener, and salt. Stir in the melted butter until the mixture begins to clump together.

3. Divide the crust mixture among the prepared muffin cups and press firmly into the bottoms.

TO MAKE THE FILLING AND ASSEMBLE:

4. In a medium bowl, beat the cream cheese with an electric mixer until smooth. Beat in the sweetener until fully incorporated.

5. Beat in the cream, lemon zest, lemon juice, and lemon extract until smooth. If desired, add yellow food coloring just a drop or two at a time until a lemon-yellow color is achieved.

6. Divide the filling mixture among the prepared muffin cups, filling each cup almost to the top, and smooth the tops. Tap the pan firmly on the counter to release any air bubbles.

7. Place the muffin pan in the freezer until the filling is firm, about 2 hours. Peel the parchment or silicone liners away from the cheesecakes and place in the refrigerator until ready to serve.

NUTRITIONAL INFORMATION

CALORIES: 223 | FAT: 20.1g | PROTEIN: 4g | CARBS: 3.9g | FIBER: 1.1g | ERYTHRITOL: 17.5g

SERVING SUGGESTION: *Garnish with a little Whipped Cream (page 164) and some lemon slices and grated lemon zest.*

STORAGE INSTRUCTIONS: *Keep the cheesecakes refrigerated for up to a week or wrap them individually and freeze for up to a month.*

TIRAMISU SHEET CAKE

Yield: One 11 by 17-inch cake (20 servings)
Prep Time: 25 minutes
Cook Time: 22 minutes

Please don't look at this long ingredient list and multi-step process and panic. I promise that this is an incredibly easy cake to put together. But it's also a great one for serving a large party and makes a perfect special-occasion dessert.

CAKE:

2 cups (200g) blanched almond flour

¾ cup granulated erythritol-based sweetener

⅓ cup (37g) coconut flour

⅓ cup unflavored whey protein powder

1 tablespoon baking powder

½ teaspoon salt

¾ cup unsweetened almond milk

½ cup (1 stick) unsalted butter, melted but not hot

3 large eggs

1 teaspoon vanilla extract

¼ cup espresso or strong brewed coffee, cooled

1 tablespoon dark rum (optional)

MASCARPONE FROSTING:

8 ounces mascarpone cheese, softened

4 ounces cream cheese (½ cup), softened

½ cup powdered erythritol-based sweetener

1 teaspoon vanilla extract

½ to ⅔ cup heavy whipping cream, room temperature

GARNISH:

1 tablespoon cocoa powder

1 ounce sugar-free dark chocolate

TO MAKE THE CAKE:

1. Preheat the oven to 325°F and thoroughly grease an 11 by 17-inch sheet pan.

2. In a medium bowl, whisk together the almond flour, sweetener, coconut flour, protein powder, baking powder, and salt. Add the almond milk, melted butter, eggs, and vanilla extract and whisk until smooth.

3. Spread the batter in the greased sheet pan and smooth the top. Bake for 18 to 22 minutes, until the edges are golden brown and the cake is set. Remove from the oven and let cool in the pan.

4. In a small bowl, combine the espresso and rum, if using. Brush over the cooled cake.

TO MAKE THE FROSTING:

5. In a large bowl, beat the mascarpone and cream cheese with an electric mixer until smooth. Beat in the sweetener and vanilla extract.

6. Add ½ cup of the cream and beat until smooth. Add more cream as needed to thin the frosting to a spreadable consistency. Spread the frosting over the cooled cake.

TO GARNISH THE CAKE:

7. Dust the top of the cake with the cocoa powder. Grate the dark chocolate over the top.

NUTRITIONAL INFORMATION

CALORIES: 238 | FAT: 21.2g | PROTEIN: 6.3g | CARBS: 5.1g | FIBER: 2.3g | ERYTHRITOL: 15g

STORAGE INSTRUCTIONS: *This cake should be stored in the fridge and will last for up to 5 days. It's best served at room temperature.*

TIP: *The cake portion of this recipe is pretty standard. If you omit the coffee and rum, it becomes a basic yellow sheet cake. Feel free to frost it with anything you like!*

SWEETENER OPTIONS: The frosting really relies on a powdered bulk sweetener for the best consistency. The cake can be sweetened with your preferred sweetener.

SLOW COOKER CHOCOLATE CAKE

OPTION

Yield: 10 servings
Prep Time: 10 minutes
Cook Time: 2½ hours

If you've never baked in a slow cooker before, you are in for a treat. It results in an incredibly moist cake that is so dense and rich that it needs no frosting. This cake doesn't come out of the slow cooker in one piece, so be prepared to serve it like a snack cake, in individual slices.

1 cup plus 2 tablespoons (113g) blanched almond flour

½ cup granulated erythritol-based sweetener

⅓ cup cocoa powder

1½ teaspoons baking powder

¼ teaspoon salt

3 large eggs

6 tablespoons (¾ stick) unsalted butter, melted but not hot

⅔ cup unsweetened almond milk

¾ teaspoon vanilla extract

⅓ cup sugar-free chocolate chips (optional)

1. Grease the insert of a 6-quart slow cooker well. You can use a smaller slow cooker, but your cake will take longer to cook through.

2. In a medium bowl, whisk together the almond flour, sweetener, cocoa powder, baking powder, and salt. Using a rubber spatula, stir in the eggs, melted butter, almond milk, and vanilla extract until well combined, then stir in the chocolate chips, if using.

3. Pour the batter into the greased slow cooker and cook on low for 2 to 2½ hours. It will be gooey and like a pudding cake at 2 hours, and more cakey and cooked through at 2½ hours.

4. Turn off the slow cooker and let the cake cool for 20 to 30 minutes, then cut into pieces and serve warm.

Special equipment:

6-quart slow cooker

SWEETENER OPTIONS:
You can get away with using any sweetener you like in this cake.

DAIRY-FREE OPTION: *Use avocado oil or melted coconut oil in place of the butter.*

SERVING SUGGESTION: *This cake is good on its own, but if you want to gild the lily, try some Whipped Cream (page 164), Vanilla Bean Semifreddo (page 124), or Chocolate Peanut Butter Sauce (page 174).*

STORAGE INSTRUCTIONS: *This cake will last for up to 5 days in the fridge.*

NUTRITIONAL INFORMATION
CALORIES: 195 | FAT: 16.7g | PROTEIN: 5.8g | CARBS: 7.4g | FIBER: 4.6g | ERYTHRITOL: 13g

FUNFETTI MUG CAKES

OPTION

Yield: 2 cakes (1 per serving)

Prep Time: 5 minutes (not including time to make sprinkles)

Cook Time: 20 minutes

½ cup (50g) blanched almond flour

2 tablespoons granulated erythritol-based sweetener

½ teaspoon baking powder

Pinch of salt

1 large egg white

2 tablespoons unsalted butter, melted but not hot

1 tablespoon water

½ teaspoon vanilla extract

1 tablespoon Coconut Sprinkles (page 175)

SWEETENER OPTIONS: Feel free to sweeten this cake with your preferred sweetener.

These mug cakes are so fun and easy, but I found that they had a better consistency when baked rather than microwaved. That said, you can easily pop them in the microwave, too.

1. Preheat the oven to 350°F and grease two 4-ounce ramekins or ovenproof mugs.

2. In a medium bowl, whisk together the almond flour, sweetener, baking powder, and salt. Stir in the egg white, melted butter, water, and vanilla extract until well combined.

3. Stir in the coconut sprinkles and divide the batter evenly between the ramekins. Bake for 18 to 20 minutes, until the tops are golden and the cakes are set to the touch.

4. Let cool for 5 minutes, then eat straight from the ramekins or flip each cake out onto a plate to serve.

DAIRY-FREE OPTION: *Use avocado oil or melted coconut oil in place of the butter.*

MICROWAVE INSTRUCTIONS: *Use microwave-safe ramekins or mugs and microwave on high power for 1 to 2 minutes, until the cakes have puffed up and are firm to the touch.*

SERVING SUGGESTION: *Top with a little Whipped Cream (page 164) and a few more coconut sprinkles.*

NUTRITIONAL INFORMATION

CALORIES: 213 | FAT: 19.4g | PROTEIN: 5.1g | CARBS: 4.4g | FIBER: 1.8g | ERYTHRITOL: 15g

DUTCH BUTTER CAKE

Yield: One 9-inch cake (8 servings)
Prep Time: 15 minutes
Cook Time: 30 minutes
Inactive Time: 1 hour

This is a dessert with an identity complex. It's a low-carb version of the classic Dutch *boterkoek,* but it's not really like a cake. It's more like a rich buttery cookie baked in a pie pan. But hey, who am I to judge? If they call it a cake, I will call it a cake, too.

⅔ cup powdered erythritol-based sweetener

½ cup (1 stick) unsalted butter, softened

1 teaspoon almond extract

1 large egg, lightly beaten, divided

1½ cups (150g) blanched almond flour

½ teaspoon baking powder

½ teaspoon salt

1 tablespoon sliced almonds

> **SWEETENER OPTIONS:**
> This cake relies on a powdered bulk sweetener for the right consistency.

1. Preheat the oven to 350°F and grease a 9-inch glass or ceramic pie pan.

2. In a large bowl, beat the sweetener, butter, and almond extract with an electric mixer until well combined. Add all but 2 teaspoons of the egg and beat in. Add the almond flour, baking powder, and salt and beat until just combined. The batter will be quite thick.

3. Spread the batter in the greased pie pan and smooth the top. Brush the remaining egg over the top. Sprinkle with the sliced almonds or arrange the almonds in a decorative pattern.

4. Bake the cake for 25 to 30 minutes, until puffed and golden brown. It will still be very soft.

5. Remove from the oven and let cool completely in the pan. Refrigerate for at least 1 hour to firm up if you want to cut the cake into proper slices. It's also wonderful scooped out of the pan like a gooey butter cake.

SERVING SUGGESTION: *Top with Whipped Cream (page 164), if desired.*

STORAGE INSTRUCTIONS: *After the initial chilling, this cake can stay out on the counter for up to 3 days. It can also remain in the fridge for up to 5 days.*

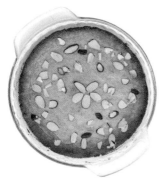

NUTRITIONAL INFORMATION

CALORIES: 240 | FAT: 22.1g | PROTEIN: 5.6g | CARBS: 4.9g | FIBER: 2.3g | ERYTHRITOL: 19.3g

ORANGE CARDAMOM BUNDT CAKE

Yield: One Bundt cake (12 servings)
Prep Time: 10 minutes
Cook Time: 50 minutes

3 cups (300g) blanched almond flour

⅔ cup granulated erythritol-based sweetener

¼ cup egg white protein powder

1 tablespoon ground cardamom

2 teaspoons baking powder

½ teaspoon salt

3 large eggs

½ cup avocado oil

¼ cup water

2 tablespoons grated orange zest

¼ cup fresh orange juice

1 teaspoon orange extract

½ teaspoon vanilla extract

Powdered erythritol-based sweetener, for dusting

SWEETENER OPTIONS: A bulk sweetener will give this cake a better consistency.

A fluted or decorative pan goes a long way toward making your cakes look elegant from the get-go. But don't panic if you don't have a Bundt pan; a 9-inch round cake pan will do just fine, and the powdered sweetener will make it look pretty.

1. Preheat the oven to 325°F and thoroughly grease a 10- to 12-cup Bundt pan.

2. In a large bowl, whisk together the almond flour, granulated sweetener, protein powder, cardamom, baking powder, and salt.

3. Using a rubber spatula, stir in the eggs, oil, water, orange zest, orange juice, and extracts until well combined. Scoop the batter into the greased Bundt pan and smooth the top.

4. Bake the cake for 40 to 50 minutes, until golden brown and firm to the touch. Let cool in the pan for 15 minutes, then gently loosen with a rubber spatula and flip out onto a wire rack to cool completely.

5. Dust with powdered sweetener before serving.

STORAGE INSTRUCTIONS: *This cake will be fine on the counter for 2 or 3 days but should be refrigerated after that. It will last for about a week in the fridge. If you wrap it up tightly, it can be frozen for up to a month.*

TIP: *The egg white protein powder isn't absolutely necessary, but it helps the cake rise and hold its shape better. If you don't need to be dairy-free, you can use whey protein powder instead. You can also try using ½ teaspoon xanthan gum to help the cake hold together without any protein powder.*

NUTRITIONAL INFORMATION
CALORIES: 237 | FAT: 24.5g | PROTEIN: 9.1g | CARBS: 7.6g | FIBER: 3.3g | ERYTHRITOL: 13.3g

PUMPKIN SPICE MUG CAKES

Yield: 2 cakes (1 per serving)
Prep Time: 3 minutes
Cook Time: 2 minutes

¼ cup pumpkin puree

3 tablespoons powdered erythritol-based sweetener

1 tablespoon avocado oil or melted coconut oil

1 tablespoon coconut flour

¼ teaspoon pumpkin pie spice

¼ teaspoon vanilla extract

1 large egg

SWEETENER OPTIONS:
Any sweetener will work in this recipe.

Pumpkin is so closely associated with fall, but the truth is that it's delicious any time of year. I always stock up on a few extra cans of pumpkin puree so I can enjoy it year-round. These easy flourless mug cakes are dense and moist, rather like pumpkin pie filling, so they should be eaten right out of the mugs.

1. In a medium bowl, whisk all of the ingredients together until well combined. Divide the batter between two 4-ounce microwave-safe ramekins or mugs.

2. Microwave on high power for 1 to 2 minutes, until the cakes are puffed and just set. Serve immediately.

SERVING SUGGESTION: *Just like pumpkin pie, these cakes are divine with a little Whipped Cream (page 164) or Coconut Whipped Cream (page 166). Sprinkle with ground cinnamon or pumpkin pie spice, if desired.*

NUTRITIONAL INFORMATION
CALORIES: 99 | FAT: 9.7g | PROTEIN: 4g | CARBS: 4.9g | FIBER: 2.2g | ERYTHRITOL: 22.5g

CHAPTER 5:

PIES AND TARTS

MOCHA CREAM PIE

Yield: One 9-inch pie (10 servings)
Prep Time: 15 minutes (not including time to make crust)
Cook Time: 5 minutes
Inactive Time: 3 hours 20 minutes

1 recipe Easy Chocolate Pie Crust (page 162)

1 cup strong brewed coffee, cooled to room temperature

1½ teaspoons grass-fed gelatin

1 cup heavy whipping cream

½ cup powdered erythritol-based sweetener

¼ cup cocoa powder

1 teaspoon vanilla extract

I have no words for how good this pie is. Wait a second; yes, I do! A creamy mocha filling in a rich chocolate crust—this is truly a special-occasion pie. It will make you look like a keto dessert rock star!

1. Lightly grease a 9-inch ceramic or glass pie pan. Press the pie crust mixture firmly and evenly into the bottom and up the sides of the greased pan. Refrigerate or freeze until the filling is ready.

2. Pour the coffee into a small saucepan and sprinkle the surface with the gelatin. Whisk to combine, then turn the heat to medium. Bring to a simmer, whisking frequently, to dissolve the gelatin. Let cool for 20 minutes.

3. In a large bowl, combine the cream, sweetener, cocoa powder, and vanilla extract. Beat with an electric mixer until it holds stiff peaks.

4. Pour in the cooled gelatin mixture and beat until blended. Spoon into the chilled crust and refrigerate until firm, about 3 hours.

SWEETENER OPTIONS: The gelatin in the filling is what helps this pie set properly, so you can use any sweetener you prefer.

TIP: *If you're not a fan of coffee flavor, substitute water for the coffee for a simple chocolate cream pie. You can also skip the crust entirely and spoon the filling into dessert cups for a delicious chocolate or mocha mousse.*

SERVING SUGGESTION: *Garnish with a little Whipped Cream (page 164) and some coffee beans.*

STORAGE INSTRUCTIONS: *This pie should be stored in the fridge and will last for up to 5 days. If you wrap it up tightly, it can be frozen for up to a month.*

NUTRITIONAL INFORMATION

CALORIES: 218 | FAT: 20.2g | PROTEIN: 4.7g | CARBS: 6.2g | FIBER: 3.1g | ERYTHRITOL: 18g

COCONUT CUSTARD PIE

OPTION

Yield: One 9-inch pie (8 servings)
Prep Time: 10 minutes
Cook Time: 50 minutes
Inactive Time: 2 hours 30 minutes

1 cup heavy whipping cream

¾ cup powdered erythritol-based sweetener

½ cup full-fat coconut milk

4 large eggs

¼ cup (½ stick) unsalted butter, melted but not hot

1¼ cups unsweetened shredded coconut, divided

3 tablespoons coconut flour

½ teaspoon baking powder

½ teaspoon vanilla extract

¼ teaspoon salt

> **SWEETENER OPTIONS:**
> A powdered bulk sweetener gives this pie the best consistency.

This crustless pie is like the best parts of a coconut cream pie: creamy, rich, and full of coconut flavor. My recipe testers gave both the dairy version and the dairy-free version a big thumbs-up!

1. Preheat the oven to 350°F and thoroughly grease a 9-inch glass or ceramic pie pan.

2. Place the cream, sweetener, coconut milk, eggs, and melted butter in a blender. Blend until well combined.

3. Add 1 cup of the shredded coconut, the coconut flour, baking powder, vanilla extract, and salt. Blend again until well combined.

4. Pour the mixture into the greased pie pan and sprinkle with the remaining ¼ cup of shredded coconut. Bake for 40 to 50 minutes, until the edges are set but the center still jiggles slightly when shaken.

5. Remove from the oven and let cool for 30 minutes, then refrigerate for 2 hours to firm up before slicing.

DAIRY-FREE OPTION: *Swap the cream and butter for full-fat coconut milk and coconut oil.*

STORAGE INSTRUCTIONS: *The creamy nature of this pie means that it needs to be refrigerated. It will last for up to 5 days.*

SERVING SUGGESTION: *I confess, I drizzled some Chocolate Peanut Butter Sauce (page 174) over a slice of this pie—and was transported straight to keto nirvana! Fresh strawberries are also a nice topping.*

NUTRITIONAL INFORMATION
CALORIES: 317 | FAT: 29.5g | PROTEIN: 5.3g | CARBS: 6.7g | FIBER: 2.6g | ERYTHRITOL: 22.5g

LEMON CURD TARTLETS

Yield: 12 tartlets (1 per serving)

Prep Time: 15 minutes (not including time to make crust)

Cook Time: 22 minutes

Inactive Time: 1 hour

CRUST:

1 recipe Easy Shortbread Crust (page 160)

LEMON CURD:

2 large eggs

⅓ cup powdered erythritol-based sweetener

3 tablespoons fresh lemon juice

2 teaspoons grated lemon zest

2½ tablespoons unsalted butter, cut into 3 pieces

GARNISH:

12 fresh raspberries

Additional powdered sweetener, for sprinkling (optional)

> **SWEETENER OPTIONS:** The curd filling is best made with a powdered bulk sweetener.

Lemon curd is actually quite easy to make—especially this version, which uses whole eggs instead of just egg yolks. Just be sure to stand over it the whole time it is on the stove, watching it carefully. When it decides to thicken up, it will do so in a flash.

TO MAKE THE CRUST:

1. Preheat the oven to 325°F and line a standard-size muffin pan with parchment paper or silicone liners.

2. Divide the shortbread crust mixture evenly among the prepared muffin cups and press firmly into the bottom and halfway up the sides of each cup.

3. Bake for 10 to 12 minutes, until the edges are just golden brown. The crusts will puff up a little as they bake. Gently press them back down after removing from the oven. Let cool completely.

TO MAKE THE LEMON CURD:

4. In a heatproof glass or ceramic bowl set over a pan of barely simmering water, whisk together the eggs, sweetener, lemon juice, and lemon zest. Whisk continuously until the mixture thickens, about 10 minutes. Watch carefully, as it will thicken all of a sudden.

5. Immediately remove from the heat and add the butter. Let sit for a few minutes to melt, then whisk until the curd is smooth and creamy.

6. Spoon the curd into the crusts and refrigerate for at least 1 hour.

TO GARNISH:

7. Top each tartlet with a raspberry and sprinkle with powdered sweetener, if desired.

NUTRITIONAL INFORMATION

CALORIES: 152 | FAT: 13.6g | PROTEIN: 4.2g | CARBS: 4g | FIBER: 1.9g | ERYTHRITOL: 11.6g

STORAGE INSTRUCTIONS: *These tartlets should be kept refrigerated. They will last for up to 5 days.*

TIP: *If twelve tartlets are too many for you, you can easily make a half batch of this recipe. Just be sure to watch that curd carefully, as the smaller quantity will cook a little faster.*

DAIRY-FREE FRUIT TARTS

Yield: Two 4-inch tarts (½ tart per serving)
Prep Time: 15 minutes (not including time to make crust or whipped cream)
Cook Time: —
Inactive Time: 1 to 2 hours

½ recipe Easy Shortbread Crust (page 160), dairy-free option

1 recipe Coconut Whipped Cream (page 166), made with coconut extract

½ cup mixed fresh berries

Fresh mint sprigs, for garnish

SWEETENER OPTIONS:
You can use any sweetener you prefer in both the crust and the filling.

These creamy fruit-topped tarts are so good, you'll never miss the dairy!

1. Lightly grease two 4-inch tart pans with removable bottoms. Divide the shortbread crust mixture between them and press firmly into the bottom and up the sides of each pan. Place the crusts in the freezer to firm up, about 15 minutes.

2. Gently loosen the crusts by pressing from the bottom and remove the sides. It will be easier to get the crusts out of the pans now before they are filled.

3. Divide the whipped cream evenly between the tarts and spread it to the edges. Refrigerate for 1 to 2 hours to firm up a bit.

4. Arrange the berries in a decorative pattern on the tops of the tarts and garnish each tart with a sprig of mint.

STORAGE INSTRUCTIONS: *These tarts should be kept in the fridge and will last for up to 5 days.*

TIP: *Why yes, you can double this recipe and make one large 9-inch tart. The filling may take a little longer to set properly. You can also make smaller tarts similar to the Lemon Curd Tartlets (page 114). This recipe will make 6 small tartlets.*

NUTRITIONAL INFORMATION
CALORIES: 306 | FAT: 28.9g | PROTEIN: 5.8g | CARBS: 8.3g | FIBER: 3g | ERYTHRITOL: 22.5g

CHOCOLATE HAZELNUT BROWNIE PIE

OPTION

Yield: One 9-inch pie (8 servings)
Prep Time: 10 minutes (not including time to make whipped cream)
Cook Time: 30 minutes
Inactive Time: 2 hours

4 ounces unsweetened chocolate, coarsely chopped

¾ cup granulated erythritol-based sweetener

½ cup boiling water

4 large eggs

½ cup (1 stick) unsalted butter, cut into tablespoons

1 teaspoon vanilla extract

1 cup (100g) hazelnut meal

GARNISH:

Whipped Cream (page 164)

Chopped toasted hazelnuts

SWEETENER OPTIONS: Really any sweetener will do here.

I love chocolate and hazelnut together almost as much as I love chocolate and peanut butter together. Which is saying a lot. This pie has a wonderful brownie-like texture—the best of all possible worlds!

1. Preheat the oven to 350°F and grease a 9-inch glass or ceramic pie pan.

2. In a food processor, pulse the coarsely chopped chocolate and sweetener until the chocolate is finely chopped. With the machine running on high, slowly pour in the boiling water until the chocolate is melted and smooth.

3. Add the eggs, butter, and vanilla extract and pulse until well combined. Add the hazelnut meal and pulse until incorporated.

4. Pour the batter into the greased pan and bake for 25 to 30 minutes, until the edges are nicely set but the middle is still a little wet-looking. Remove from the oven and let cool to room temperature, then refrigerate for 2 hours to firm up.

5. Garnish with whipped cream and toasted hazelnuts.

DAIRY-FREE OPTION: *Replace the butter with a neutral oil that won't overpower the delicate flavor of the hazelnuts, such as avocado oil or refined coconut oil. Garnish with Coconut Whipped Cream (page 166) flavored with vanilla extract, if desired.*

SERVING SUGGESTION: *Want to take this pie to a whole new level? Try drizzling some Homemade Chocolate Hazelnut Spread (page 170) on top!*

STORAGE SUGGESTIONS: *This pie will last for up to 5 days in the fridge. Wrapped tightly, it can be frozen for up to a month.*

TIP: *If you want to amp up the hazelnut flavor, try using hazelnut extract in place of the vanilla. One of my recipe testers really enjoyed the pie this way.*

NUTRITIONAL INFORMATION

CALORIES: 324 | FAT: 28.4g | PROTEIN: 7.3g | CARBS: 6.8g | FIBER: 3.9g | ERYTHRITOL: 22.5g

STRAWBERRY RHUBARB CRISP FOR TWO

OPTION

Yield: 1 small crisp (2 servings)
Prep Time: 10 minutes
Cook Time: 30 minutes

A fruit crisp is really just a pie without a bottom crust. I grew up on rhubarb crisps, and this keto version does not disappoint. It's beyond amazing with a little Vanilla Bean Semifreddo (page 124) on top.

TOPPING:

2½ tablespoons blanched almond flour

1 tablespoon unsweetened shredded coconut

1 tablespoon granulated erythritol-based sweetener

1½ teaspoons finely chopped pecans

¼ teaspoon ground cinnamon

Pinch of salt

2 teaspoons unsalted butter, melted

FILLING:

½ cup chopped fresh rhubarb

⅓ cup chopped fresh strawberries

1 tablespoon granulated erythritol-based sweetener

¹⁄₁₆ teaspoon xanthan gum

SWEETENER OPTIONS: The topping really needs a bulk erythritol-based sweetener to become crisp as it bakes. The filling can be sweetened with whichever sweetener you prefer.

TO MAKE THE TOPPING:

1. Preheat the oven to 300°F and line a baking sheet with parchment paper.

2. In a medium bowl, whisk together the almond flour, coconut, sweetener, pecans, cinnamon, and salt. Stir in the melted butter until the mixture resembles coarse crumbs.

3. Transfer the topping mixture to the lined baking sheet and press down firmly to flatten. Bake for about 15 minutes, until golden brown. Remove from the oven and let cool while you prepare the filling.

TO MAKE THE FILLING AND ASSEMBLE:

4. Preheat the oven to 400°F.

5. In a medium bowl, toss all of the filling ingredients together to combine well. Transfer to an 8-ounce ramekin and cover with foil. Bake for 10 to 15 minutes, until hot and bubbling.

6. Crumble the topping a little with your fingers and sprinkle over the filling. Serve warm.

DAIRY-FREE OPTION: *Use coconut oil or avocado oil in place of the butter.*

TIP: *You can also bake this crisp in two 4-ounce ramekins.*

NUTRITIONAL INFORMATION

CALORIES: 135 | FAT: 11.5g | PROTEIN: 2.6g | CARBS: 6.3g | FIBER: 2.6g | ERYTHRITOL: 15g

CHAPTER 6:

FROZEN DESSERTS

VANILLA BEAN SEMIFREDDO

Yield: About 3 cups (½ cup per serving)
Prep Time: 10 minutes
Cook Time: 7 minutes
Inactive Time: 6 to 8 hours

2 large eggs

3 large egg yolks

⅔ cup powdered erythritol-based sweetener, divided

1 tablespoon vodka (optional)

½ vanilla bean

1⅓ cups heavy whipping cream

½ teaspoon vanilla extract

SWEETENER OPTIONS:
You can use any sweetener you like in this recipe.

Semifreddo, or "semifrozen," is the original no-churn ice cream. It's wonderfully rich and creamy, no ice cream maker required! I like to keep some on hand at all times for when ice cream cravings strike.

1. Place the eggs, egg yolks, and ⅓ cup of the sweetener in a heatproof bowl set over a pan of barely simmering water. Whisk continuously until the mixture thickens, 5 to 7 minutes. Remove the bowl from the pan and let the mixture cool to lukewarm, whisking frequently.

2. Whisk in the vodka, if using. Slice the vanilla bean open lengthwise and scrape out the seeds using a sharp knife. Stir the vanilla seeds into the egg mixture.

3. In a large bowl, use an electric mixer to whip the cream with the remaining ⅓ cup of sweetener and the vanilla extract until it holds stiff peaks. Add the egg mixture to the whipped cream and gently fold in until no streaks remain.

4. Transfer the mixture to an airtight container and freeze until firm, 6 to 8 hours.

STORAGE INSTRUCTIONS: *This semifreddo will last for up to 6 weeks in your freezer—possibly longer, but I wouldn't know, as we always eat it much faster!*

TIPS: *The addition of a little alcohol, like vodka, keeps the semifreddo from getting too icy in the freezer. After 24 hours in the freezer, the ice cream will be very hard, but 15 minutes on the counter will allow it to soften enough for serving.*

If you don't have vanilla beans, you can simply add another ½ teaspoon of vanilla extract to the whipped cream in Step 3.

NUTRITIONAL INFORMATION
CALORIES: 245 | FAT: 22.2g | PROTEIN: 4.5g | CARBS: 2g | FIBER: 0g | ERYTHRITOL: 26.5g

SALTED CARAMEL AFFOGATO

Yield: 1 serving

Prep Time: 5 minutes (not including time to make semifreddo or caramel sauce)

Cook Time: —

½ cup Vanilla Bean Semifreddo (page 124)

2 tablespoons Salted Caramel Sauce (page 173)

1 shot freshly made espresso, or ¼ cup strong brewed coffee

If you love coffee and you love ice cream, then you will love affogato. It means "drowned" in Italian; you are drowning the ice cream in hot coffee. The addition of low-carb salted caramel sauce takes it to a whole new level. If you already have the semifreddo and the sauce made, you can put together this delicious dessert in a matter of minutes.

Place the semifreddo in a small bowl or mug and drizzle with the caramel sauce. Pour the hot coffee over the top and enjoy.

NUTRITIONAL INFORMATION

CALORIES: 358 | FAT: 32.8g | PROTEIN: 4.9g | CARBS: 5.4g | FIBER: 0g | ERYTHRITOL: 37.7g

RIDICULOUSLY EASY ROOT BEER FLOATS

OPTION

Yield: 2 servings

Prep Time: 5 minutes (not including time to make whipped cream)

Cook Time: —

Inactive Time: 1 to 2 hours

½ recipe Whipped Cream (page 164)

1 (12-ounce) can or bottle sugar-free root beer, chilled

SWEETENER OPTIONS: Use any sweetener you like in the whipped cream.

DAIRY-FREE OPTION: *Just swap out the whipped cream for a full recipe of Coconut Whipped Cream (page 166).*

TIPS: *There are several brands of root beer that are sweetened with stevia or erythritol or both, such as Virgil's Zero. I really like the Virgil's brand, and so do my kids. Zevia makes a ginger root beer, but be forewarned that it is a clear liquid. It tastes the same but doesn't look like root beer!*

You can easily use Vanilla Bean Semifreddo (page 124) in place of the frozen whipped cream.

My kids love this fun treat, and using frozen whipped cream means that you don't have to make your own low-carb vanilla ice cream. You really can't tell the difference once it's all together in the glass!

1. Line a baking sheet with wax paper or parchment paper. Drop the whipped cream by heaping spoonfuls onto the paper and freeze until firm, 1 to 2 hours.

2. Carefully peel the frozen whipped cream from the paper and divide between two 10-ounce glasses. Fill the glasses with the root beer and serve.

NUTRITIONAL INFORMATION

CALORIES: 208 | FAT: 20.8g | PROTEIN: 1.5g | CARBS: 1.7g | ERYTHRITOL: 15g

CHOCOLATE FAT BOMB
ICE CREAM

Yield: About 1 quart (½ cup per serving)
Prep Time: 30 minutes
Cook Time: 5 minutes
Inactive Time: 3 to 4 hours

2½ cups heavy whipping cream, divided

¼ cup (½ stick) unsalted butter

⅔ cup powdered erythritol-based sweetener

3 ounces unsweetened chocolate, chopped

1 teaspoon vanilla extract

Pinch of salt

2 tablespoons vodka (optional)

Special equipment:

Ice cream maker

This rich ice cream contains no eggs, but it packs a seriously chocolatey punch. If you own an ice cream maker, you will find yourself making this recipe frequently!

1. In a large saucepan over medium heat, bring 1½ cups of the cream and the butter just to a simmer, stirring, until the butter is melted.

2. Remove from the heat and add the sweetener, chocolate, vanilla extract, and salt. Let sit for about 5 minutes, until the chocolate is melted, then whisk until smooth. Let the mixture cool to room temperature.

3. Whisk in the remaining 1 cup of cream and the vodka, if using. Refrigerate until just cool to the touch, 1 to 2 hours.

4. Pour into an ice cream maker and churn according to the manufacturer's instructions. Transfer to an airtight container and freeze until firm, another 2 hours or so.

SWEETENER OPTIONS: This recipe doesn't rely on a bulk sweetener, so use any type you prefer.

STORAGE INSTRUCTIONS: *This ice cream should last for up to 2 months in an airtight container in the freezer.*

TIPS: *Don't chill the ice cream base too long or it will become too thick to churn. If you do let it chill to the point of thickening, you can just let it warm up a bit on the counter before proceeding.*

You can eat this ice cream right when it comes out of the ice cream maker, but it will be more like a soft serve than a firm ice cream.

This ice cream becomes very solid when frozen for longer than a few hours, but it softens nicely with 15 to 20 minutes on the counter. I like to portion it out into individual servings right from the ice cream maker. That way, I don't have to soften the whole batch when I'm in the mood for a chocolatey treat.

As with the Vanilla Bean Semifreddo (page 124), the vodka in this recipe keeps the ice cream from getting too icy in the freezer.

NUTRITIONAL INFORMATION
CALORIES: 381 | FAT: 36.7g | PROTEIN: 3.1g | CARBS: 5.2g | FIBER: 1.8g | ERYTHRITOL: 19.9g

FROZEN KEY LIME MINI PIES

Yield: 6 mini pies (1 per serving)
Prep Time: 20 minutes
Cook Time: 7 minutes
Inactive Time: 3 to 4 hours

I am not supposed to choose favorites; I am supposed to love all of my recipes equally. But this one ranks up there as one of my favorites in this book. There is just something so good about the tangy Key lime filling juxtaposed with the sweet and salty pecans.

4 ounces cream cheese (½ cup), softened

¼ cup plus 2 tablespoons powdered erythritol-based sweetener, divided

⅓ cup Key lime juice

½ cup heavy whipping cream

1 tablespoon butter (salted or unsalted)

½ cup finely chopped raw pecans

1 tablespoon granulated erythritol-based sweetener

¼ teaspoon salt

SWEETENER OPTIONS: The filling can be sweetened with any sweetener, but the pecans are best made with a bulk erythritol-based sweetener.

1. Line 6 standard-size muffin cups with parchment paper or silicone liners.

2. In a medium bowl, beat the cream cheese and ¼ cup of the powdered sweetener with an electric mixer until smooth. Beat in the lime juice.

3. In another bowl, beat the cream with the remaining 2 tablespoons of powdered sweetener until it holds stiff peaks. Fold the whipped cream into the cream cheese mixture until well combined. Divide the mixture among the lined muffin cups, filling each cup almost to the top.

4. Melt the butter in a small skillet over medium heat. Add the pecans and granulated sweetener and cook for 5 to 7 minutes, until the pecans are toasted and fragrant. Sprinkle with the salt, then remove from the heat and let cool for 5 minutes.

5. Sprinkle the pecan mixture over the lime mixture in the muffin cups, pressing lightly to adhere.

6. Freeze for 3 to 4 hours, until set. Invert the pies onto a plate and remove the liners before serving.

SERVING SUGGESTION: *Garnish with a little Whipped Cream (page 164) and some lime slices.*

STORAGE INSTRUCTIONS: *These little treats will last for several weeks in the freezer.*

TIPS: *Those little Key limes are a pain to squeeze to get enough juice. I found bottled Key lime juice, but feel free to use regular limes instead.*

These mini pies become very hard if frozen for longer than about 6 hours, but they soften nicely with 15 minutes on the counter.

NUTRITIONAL INFORMATION

CALORIES: 219 | FAT: 20.5g | PROTEIN: 2.4g | CARBS: 3.7g | FIBER: 0.9g | ERYTHRITOL: 17.5g

STRAWBERRY CHEESECAKE POPS

OPTION

Yield: 6 pops (1 per serving)
Prep Time: 10 minutes
Cook Time: —
Inactive Time: 4 hours

4 ounces cream cheese
(½ cup), softened

½ cup heavy whipping cream

¼ cup plus 2 tablespoons
powdered erythritol-based
sweetener

1 teaspoon grated lemon zest

2 teaspoons fresh lemon juice

1 cup chopped strawberries,
divided

Special equipment:

6 (3-ounce) ice pop molds

> **SWEETENER OPTIONS:**
> Anything goes in this easy
> and adaptable recipe!

These creamy ice pops are my favorite easy summer treat!

1. Place the cream cheese in a food processor or high-powered blender and process until smooth.

2. Add the cream, sweetener, lemon zest, and lemon juice. Process until well combined.

3. Add ¾ cup of the strawberries and process until almost fully smooth. Stir in the remaining chopped strawberries.

4. Pour the mixture into the ice pop molds and push a stick about two-thirds of the way into each mold. I recommend using wooden sticks, which tend to grip the mixture better and don't come out when you are trying to unmold the pops.

5. Freeze for at least 4 hours. To unmold, run under hot water for 20 to 30 seconds, then twist the stick gently to release.

DAIRY-FREE OPTION: *You can make a very good dairy-free version using Kite Hill's almond milk cream cheese and some coconut milk in place of the heavy whipping cream.*

STORAGE INSTRUCTIONS: *These pops will last for up to 2 months in the freezer. If you take them out of the molds, just place them in a large resealable bag and squeeze all the air out so they don't get freezer burn.*

TIP: *I like to boil water in my tea kettle and run it over the ice pop molds to release them. This way, I don't waste water waiting for the tap to come to temperature.*

NUTRITIONAL INFORMATION
CALORIES: 145 | FAT: 12.7g | PROTEIN: 1.7g | CARBS: 3.6g | FIBER: 0.6g | ERYTHRITOL: 15g

COCONUT MILK FUDGE POPS

Yield: 6 pops (1 per serving)
Prep Time: 10 minutes
Cook Time: 5 minutes
Inactive Time: 6 hours

1 (13.5-ounce) can full-fat coconut milk

⅓ cup cocoa powder

⅓ cup powdered erythritol-based sweetener

Pinch of salt

1½ teaspoons vanilla extract

Special equipment:

6 (3-ounce) ice pop molds

These frozen treats are so fudgy and rich, you'd never know they are dairy-free and low-carb!

1. In a medium saucepan over medium heat, whisk together the coconut milk, cocoa powder, sweetener, and salt. Bring to a simmer, whisking continuously until the mixture is uniform.

2. Simmer for 4 to 5 minutes, whisking frequently, until thickened. Whisk in the vanilla extract and let cool for 10 minutes. Pour into the ice pop molds.

3. Freeze for 1 hour, then push a stick about two-thirds of the way into each mold. I recommend using wooden sticks, which tend to grip the mixture better and don't come out when you are trying to unmold the pops.

4. Freeze until solid, at least 5 more hours. To unmold, run under hot water for 20 to 30 seconds, then twist the stick gently to release.

SWEETENER OPTIONS: The powdered bulk sweetener helps thicken the fudge pop base, so it's your best option here. However, you can use another sweetener if you prefer.

STORAGE INSTRUCTIONS: *These fudge pops will last for up to 2 months in the freezer. If you take them out of the molds, just place them in a large resealable bag and squeeze all the air out so they don't get freezer burn.*

TIP: *Even after hours in the freezer, these pops can melt quickly. I recommend freezing them overnight for the best results.*

NUTRITIONAL INFORMATION

CALORIES: 137 | FAT: 12.9g | PROTEIN: 2.2g | CARBS: 4.6g | FIBER: 1.8g | ERYTHRITOL: 13.3g

CHAPTER 7

CUSTARD, MOUSSE, AND OTHER DELICIOUS DESSERTS

BUTTERSCOTCH PUDDING

OPTION

Yield: 6 servings
Prep Time: 10 minutes
Cook Time: 18 minutes
Inactive Time: 3 hours

½ cup (1 stick) salted butter, divided

2 teaspoons yacón syrup or molasses (for flavor and color)

¾ cup powdered erythritol-based sweetener

1 cup heavy whipping cream

1 cup unsweetened almond milk

1 tablespoon whiskey (optional)

4 large egg yolks

1 teaspoon butterscotch or caramel extract

½ teaspoon vanilla extract

½ teaspoon xanthan gum

> **SWEETENER OPTIONS:**
> Using a powdered bulk sweetener helps this pudding set properly.

You just can't argue with the rich flavor of butterscotch. This pudding is so decadent, you could easily divide it into eight servings instead of six.

1. Heat 6 tablespoons of the butter in a medium saucepan over medium heat until it turns a light amber color, about 4 minutes.

2. Whisk in the yacón syrup, then slowly add the sweetener, whisking continuously. Slowly add the cream and almond milk, whisking continuously, and bring to a simmer. Remove from the heat and stir in the whiskey, if using.

3. In a medium bowl, whisk the egg yolks until smooth. Slowly add about 1 cup of the hot cream mixture to the yolks, whisking continuously. Then slowly whisk the egg mixture back into the remaining cream in the saucepan.

4. Return the pan to medium heat and cook, whisking continuously, until the pudding bubbles and begins to thicken, 5 to 10 minutes. Remove from the heat and add the remaining 2 tablespoons of butter and the extracts. Let the butter melt, then whisk it in.

5. Sprinkle the surface of the pudding with the xanthan gum and whisk quickly to combine. Use a spatula to scrape the bottom and sides of the pan and whisk until very smooth.

6. Divide the pudding among 6 dessert cups and refrigerate until set, about 3 hours.

NUT-FREE OPTION: *Use unsweetened hemp milk in place of the almond milk.*

SERVING SUGGESTION: *Top with a little Whipped Cream (page 164).*

TIP: *Using just a little yacón syrup or molasses enhances the flavor and color of the pudding and adds only about 1 gram of carbs per serving. You can skip it, but your pudding will be a lot lighter.*

NUTRITIONAL INFORMATION
CALORIES: 328 | FAT: 31.5g | PROTEIN: 2.9g | CARBS: 3g | FIBER: 0.2g | ERYTHRITOL: 30g

DAIRY-FREE
PEANUT BUTTER MOUSSE

Yield: 6 servings
Prep Time: 10 minutes
Cook Time: —
Inactive Time: 2 hours

¼ cup plus 2 tablespoons creamy peanut butter (salted)

2 tablespoons coconut oil, slightly softened

1 (13.5-ounce) can full-fat coconut milk, refrigerated overnight

¼ cup powdered erythritol-based sweetener

½ teaspoon vanilla extract

SWEETENER OPTIONS:
This mousse sets best when you use a powdered bulk sweetener, but you could probably get away with another sweetener.

Peanut butter mousse is a low-carb classic, but it's usually made with cream cheese and heavy whipping cream. This dairy-free version will have your taste buds dancing!

1. In a medium bowl, beat the peanut butter and coconut oil with an electric mixer until well combined.

2. Skim the solid portion (or coconut cream) from the top of the can of coconut milk into the bowl and beat until incorporated. Discard the thinner coconut water or reserve it for another use. Beat in the sweetener and vanilla extract.

3. Spoon the mousse into 6 small dessert cups or glasses and refrigerate until firm, at least 2 hours.

NUTRITIONAL INFORMATION
CALORIES: 219 | FAT: 20g | PROTEIN: 4.8g | CARBS: 5.3g | FIBER: 0.8g | ERYTHRITOL: 10g

MASCARPONE MOUSSE WITH ROASTED STRAWBERRIES

Yield: 6 servings
Prep Time: 15 minutes
Cook Time: 20 minutes

ROASTED STRAWBERRIES:

2 cups quartered strawberries

2 teaspoons granulated erythritol-based sweetener

¼ teaspoon vanilla extract

MASCARPONE MOUSSE:

8 ounces mascarpone cheese, softened

4 ounces cream cheese (½ cup), softened

¼ cup plus 2 tablespoons powdered erythritol-based sweetener, divided

1 teaspoon vanilla extract

1 cup heavy whipping cream

SWEETENER OPTIONS: Use any sweetener you prefer in both the roasted strawberries and the mousse.

This mousse is pretty great on its own, but it becomes something almost magical with the addition of roasted strawberries.

TO ROAST THE STRAWBERRIES:

1. Preheat the oven to 375°F and lightly grease a medium-size baking dish.

2. Place the strawberries in the greased dish and sprinkle with the granulated sweetener. Add the vanilla extract and toss to combine, then spread out in the pan.

3. Roast for 20 minutes, until the berries are soft and tender and have released much of their juice. While the berries are roasting, make the mousse.

TO MAKE THE MOUSSE AND ASSEMBLE:

4. In a large bowl, beat the mascarpone, cream cheese, ¼ cup of the powdered sweetener, and the vanilla extract with an electric mixer until well combined.

5. In another bowl, beat the cream with the remaining 2 tablespoons of powdered sweetener until it holds stiff peaks. Fold the whipped cream into the mascarpone mixture until combined.

6. Pipe or spoon the mousse into 6 small dessert cups. Top with the roasted strawberries and serve immediately.

TIP: *Mascarpone has a naturally sweet taste even though it has no carbs, so it doesn't need much sweetener to make it taste like a real treat.*

NUTRITIONAL INFORMATION
CALORIES: 386 | FAT: 37.1g | PROTEIN: 5g | CARBS: 6.2g | FIBER: 1.1g | ERYTHRITOL: 16.5g

CHOCOLATE HAZELNUT MOUSSE

Yield: 6 servings

Prep Time: 10 minutes (not including time to make chocolate hazelnut spread)

Cook Time: —

¼ cup (½ stick) unsalted butter, softened

½ cup Homemade Chocolate Hazelnut Spread (page 170), room temperature

⅓ cup powdered erythritol-based sweetener

½ to ⅔ cup heavy whipping cream, divided

½ teaspoon hazelnut or vanilla extract

SWEETENER OPTIONS: This recipe absolutely requires a powdered bulk sweetener to achieve the right consistency.

Have I ever told you that I love chocolate and hazelnut together? Oh yes, I may have mentioned that in passing a few billion times already. This Nutella-like mousse is the stuff of my dreams. Fair warning: it's insanely rich!

1. In a medium bowl, cream the butter with an electric mixer until smooth. Add the chocolate hazelnut spread and sweetener and beat until well combined.

2. Add ½ cup of the cream and the hazelnut extract and beat until smooth. If the mixture is very thick, add the remaining cream and beat until smooth.

3. Pipe or spoon the mousse into 6 dessert cups. Serve immediately or chill until ready to serve. If you chill the mousse, let it sit out on the counter for a few minutes to soften before serving.

SERVING SUGGESTION: *Top the mousse with some roasted, husked hazelnuts.*

TIP: *The smoothness of this mousse really depends on how smooth you can get your chocolate hazelnut spread. A good high-powered blender or food processor goes a long way here. But the mousse is delicious no matter how smooth it is!*

NUTRITIONAL INFORMATION

CALORIES: 267 | FAT: 26.7g | PROTEIN: 2.7g | CARBS: 3.7g | FIBER: 1.8g | ERYTHRITOL: 18.3g

LEMON CURD MOUSSE

Yield: 4 servings
Prep Time: 5 minutes (not including time to make curd or whipped cream)
Cook Time: —
Inactive Time: 1 hour

1 recipe Lemon Curd (page 114)
¾ recipe Whipped Cream (page 164) (see Tip)

This is a wonderful tart-sweet lemon dessert. Be sure to chill the lemon curd properly before you proceed with the recipe so that you don't melt your freshly whipped cream!

1. After preparing the lemon curd according to the recipe for the Lemon Curd Tartlets, cover with plastic wrap and press it flush to the surface. Chill for at least 1 hour.

2. Fold the lemon curd and whipped cream together until no streaks remain. Pipe or spoon the mousse into 4 dessert cups and serve immediately or chill until ready to serve.

SWEETENER OPTIONS: This mousse will have better structure and consistency if you use a powdered bulk sweetener in both the lemon curd and the whipped cream.

SERVING SUGGESTION: *Top the mousse with a little more whipped cream and some lemon slices or zest or both. Or try it with some berries on top.*

TIP: *Use Stabilized Whipped Cream (page 165) if you need to let the mousse sit out for a bit before serving.*

NUTRITIONAL INFORMATION
CALORIES: 262 | FAT: 24.5g | PROTEIN: 4.2g | CARBS: 2.5g | FIBER: 0.1g | ERYTHRITOL: 26.3g

RASPBERRY FOOL

OPTION

Yield: 4 servings

Prep Time: 15 minutes (not including time to make whipped cream)

Cook Time: —

1 cup frozen raspberries, thawed

2 to 4 tablespoons powdered erythritol-based sweetener, divided

1 recipe Whipped Cream (page 164)

Fresh berries, for garnish

SWEETENER OPTIONS: You can sweeten this dessert with any sweetener you prefer.

The simplicity of this dessert belies its utter deliciousness. It's really just slightly sweetened raspberry puree folded into whipped cream, but it tastes like a tart-sweet berry cloud. You can make it with any berry variety you like.

1. In a blender or food processor, process the berries and 2 tablespoons of the sweetener until smooth. Add up to 2 tablespoons more sweetener to taste.

2. Gently fold the raspberry puree into the whipped cream, leaving some streaks. Spoon the mixture into 4 dessert cups. Serve immediately or refrigerate until ready to serve. Garnish with fresh berries before serving.

DAIRY-FREE OPTION: *Use a double batch of Coconut Whipped Cream (page 166).*

TIPS: *Try using Stabilized Whipped Cream (page 165) if you need to make this recipe ahead of time. It will even be able to stand at room temperature for a few hours that way.*

This is an easy dessert to make for two people. Simply halve everything and proceed as directed. You can also double or triple the recipe for a crowd.

NUTRITIONAL INFORMATION
CALORIES: 226 | FAT: 20.1g | PROTEIN: 1.7g | CARBS: 5.2g | FIBER: 1g | ERYTHRITOL: 15g

CANNOLI DESSERT DIP

Yield: 8 servings

Prep Time: 10 minutes

Cook Time: —

1 cup whole-milk ricotta cheese, room temperature

6 ounces cream cheese (¾ cup), softened

¾ cup powdered erythritol-based sweetener, plus more for sprinkling

½ teaspoon vanilla extract

½ cup heavy whipping cream

⅓ cup sugar-free chocolate chips

SWEETENER OPTIONS: Sweeten this dip with your choice of sweetener.

Dessert dips are fun for parties and get-togethers. But you just might find that you don't want to share . . .

1. In a blender or food processor, blend the ricotta, cream cheese, sweetener, and vanilla extract until smooth.

2. In a medium bowl, whip the cream with an electric mixer until it holds stiff peaks. Gently fold in the ricotta mixture and most of the chocolate chips, reserving a few to sprinkle on top.

3. Sprinkle lightly with more powdered sweetener and the remaining chocolate chips and serve.

SERVING SUGGESTION: *Serve with fresh berries or Slice-and-Bake Vanilla Wafers (page 60). Or pipe the dip into Chocolate Dessert Cups (page 176) to make individual little cannoli treats.*

STORAGE INSTRUCTIONS: *This dip will keep in the refrigerator for up to 5 days.*

TIP: *Some brands of ricotta are grainier than others. Whipping this dip in a blender or food processor will make it smoother, but you can also simply beat the ingredients together in a bowl before folding in the whipped cream.*

NUTRITIONAL INFORMATION

CALORIES: 219 | FAT: 17.9g | PROTEIN: 5.7g | CARBS: 5.6g | FIBER: 1.3g | ERYTHRITOL: 22.5g

SLOW COOKER
COFFEE COCONUT CUSTARD

Yield: 4 servings
Prep Time: 5 minutes
Cook Time: 2 hours
Inactive Time: 2 hours

1 cup plus 2 tablespoons
full-fat coconut milk

1 large egg

2 large egg yolks

½ teaspoon vanilla extract

½ cup powdered erythritol-
based sweetener

1 teaspoon espresso powder

Special equipment:

5- or 6-quart slow cooker

> **SWEETENER OPTIONS:**
> This custard sets best when
> you use a powdered bulk
> sweetener, but you can try
> another type if you prefer.

A slow cooker is an ideal way to bake custard, as the gentle heat and moist atmosphere cook the mixture to creamy perfection.

1. In a medium bowl, whisk together all of the ingredients until the espresso powder has dissolved and everything is well combined.

2. Divide the mixture among four 4-ounce ramekins or small coffee cups and set the ramekins inside a 5- or 6-quart slow cooker.

3. Add enough water to the slow cooker to come halfway up the sides of the ramekins, taking care not to get any water in the custard.

4. Cook on high for 1½ to 2 hours, until the custard is mostly set but the centers still jiggle slightly.

5. Remove and let cool to room temperature, then refrigerate for 2 hours before serving.

SERVING SUGGESTION: *Dollop with a little Coconut Whipped Cream (page 166) and garnish with a coffee bean.*

NUTRITIONAL INFORMATION
CALORIES: 186 | FAT: 16.8g | PROTEIN: 4.3g | CARBS: 2.6g | FIBER: 0g | ERYTHRITOL: 30g

COCONUT LIME PANNA COTTA

Yield: **4 servings**
Prep Time: **10 minutes**
Cook Time: **5 minutes**
Inactive Time: **3 hours**

1 (13.5-ounce) can full-fat coconut milk, divided

1½ teaspoons grass-fed gelatin

⅓ cup powdered erythritol-based sweetener

1 teaspoon grated lime zest

2 tablespoons fresh lime juice

¼ teaspoon coconut extract

SWEETENER OPTIONS:
The gelatin is the main setting component for panna cotta, so you should be able to use any sweetener you like for this recipe.

Panna cotta is such an easy dessert to make, and it's wonderfully creamy and smooth. Be sure to heat the coconut milk mixture very gently; too much heat and it can separate as it cools, leaving a funny layer of coconut oil on top.

1. Lightly grease four 4-ounce ramekins.

2. In a medium saucepan over medium-low heat, whisk half of the coconut milk with the gelatin. Bring just to a simmer, whisking to dissolve the gelatin in the milk.

3. Remove from the heat and add the remaining coconut milk, sweetener, lime zest, lime juice, and coconut extract. Whisk to combine well and dissolve the sweetener.

4. Divide the mixture among the greased ramekins and chill until set, about 3 hours.

5. To unmold, set the ramekins in a bowl of hot water for 20 to 30 seconds. Set a plate upside down on top of each ramekin and flip the whole thing over. You may need to give it a good shake to free it. You can also eat the panna cotta straight from the ramekins.

TIP: *To keep this dessert totally dairy-free, use coconut oil or coconut oil spray for greasing the ramekins.*

SERVING SUGGESTION: *Garnish the panna cotta with a little lime zest or some lime slices or both.*

NUTRITIONAL INFORMATION
CALORIES: 190 | FAT: 18.5g | PROTEIN: 2.6g | CARBS: 3.2g | FIBER: 0g | ERYTHRITOL: 19.9g

CHOCOLATE COBBLER

OPTION

Yield: 8 servings
Prep Time: 10 minutes
Cook Time: 40 minutes

Rich and deeply chocolatey, this cobbler is my low-carb take on a classic Southern recipe. It has a crispy top layer and a gooey chocolate underlayer. It may not look very pretty in the pan, but then some of the ugliest foods are also the tastiest. A little Whipped Cream (page 164) or Vanilla Bean Semifreddo (page 124) will make it all the more appealing.

CHOCOLATE LAYER:

1¼ cups blanched almond flour

⅓ cup granulated erythritol-based sweetener

¼ cup cocoa powder

3 tablespoons unflavored whey protein powder

2 teaspoons baking powder

½ teaspoon espresso powder (optional)

¼ teaspoon salt

½ cup heavy whipping cream

¼ cup (½ stick) unsalted butter, melted

TOPPING:

2 tablespoons granulated erythritol-based sweetener

1 tablespoon cocoa powder

¾ cup hot water

SWEETENER OPTIONS:
You really need a granulated bulk sweetener for the top layer to get the right crunchiness. The chocolate layer can be sweetened with your preferred sweetener.

1. Preheat the oven to 325°F.

2. Make the chocolate layer: In a large bowl, whisk together the almond flour, sweetener, cocoa powder, protein powder, baking powder, espresso powder (if using), and salt. Stir in the cream and melted butter until thoroughly combined. Spread the mixture evenly in an 8-inch square baking dish.

3. Make the topping: In a small bowl, whisk together the sweetener and cocoa powder. Sprinkle evenly over the cobbler. Pour the hot water over the cobbler; do not stir.

4. Bake for 35 to 40 minutes, until set in the middle. The cobbler will puff up while baking but will sink back down by the end.

5. Remove from the oven and let cool for 10 to 15 minutes, then serve warm out of the baking dish.

DAIRY-FREE OPTION: *Use collagen powder (or peptides) instead of whey protein powder, coconut milk instead of cream, and coconut oil or avocado oil in place of the butter.*

STORAGE INSTRUCTIONS: *This cobbler will last in the fridge for up to a week. Rewarm it gently in the oven or microwave.*

TIP: *Using a little coffee in a recipe such as this enhances the chocolate flavor. You can leave it out, but just know that it doesn't actually make the dessert taste like coffee or mocha.*

NUTRITIONAL INFORMATION
CALORIES: 223 | FAT: 20g | PROTEIN: 6.5g | CARBS: 7.1g | FIBER: 3.4g | ERYTHRITOL: 13.7g

CHAPTER 8:

EXTRAS

EASY SHORTBREAD CRUST

OPTION

Yield: One 9-inch pie crust or
9-inch square crust (10 servings)
Prep Time: 5 minutes
Cook Time: —

1½ cups (150g) blanched
almond flour

¼ cup powdered erythritol-
based sweetener

½ teaspoon salt

¼ cup (½ stick) unsalted
butter, melted

This versatile crust can be used for pies, tarts, and bars. It
can be baked or filled unbaked, frozen ahead of time, and even
made dairy-free.

1. In a medium bowl, whisk together the almond flour,
   sweetener, and salt. Stir in the melted butter until the
   mixture begins to clump together.

2. Prepare as directed for the recipe you are following.

SWEETENER OPTIONS:
I find that this recipe works
best with a powdered bulk
sweetener. If you use a
non-bulk sweetener, you
may need to add an extra
tablespoon or two of
almond flour to make up
for the bulk. Do not use a
granulated sweetener; it
would be too gritty in this
no-bake application.

DAIRY-FREE OPTION: *Use melted coconut oil or avocado oil in place of
the butter.*

STORAGE INSTRUCTIONS: *You can easily make this crust a day or
two ahead and store it in the fridge. Just be sure to shape it into the pan
for your intended recipe and wrap it tightly in plastic wrap so it doesn't
dry out too much. You can bake it straight from the fridge. You can also
freeze it for several weeks, but be sure to let it thaw before baking.*

TIP: *If your recipe calls for a prebaked crust, simply bake this crust at
325°F for 10 to 12 minutes, until the edges are just golden brown.*

NUTRITIONAL INFORMATION (crust only):
CALORIES: 137 | FAT: 12.7g | PROTEIN: 3.7g | CARBS: 3.6g | FIBER: 1.8g | ERYTHRITOL: 6g

EASY CHOCOLATE PIE CRUST

OPTION

Yield: One 9-inch pie crust or
9-inch square crust (10 servings)
Prep Time: 5 minutes
Cook Time: —

Like the shortbread crust on page 160, this chocolate crust is extremely versatile for keto dessert recipes. In this book, I have paired it with a mocha cream filling (see page 110), but it can also be used for bars and other desserts. See "Mix-and-Match Desserts" on page 34 for another idea, or simply let your imagination run wild!

1¼ cups (125g) blanched almond flour

¼ cup cocoa powder

¼ cup powdered erythritol-based sweetener

¼ teaspoon salt

¼ cup (½ stick) unsalted butter, melted

1 tablespoon water

1. In a medium bowl, whisk together the almond flour, cocoa powder, sweetener, and salt. Add the melted butter and water and stir until the mixture begins to clump together.

2. Prepare as directed for the recipe you are following.

DAIRY-FREE OPTION: *Use melted coconut oil or avocado oil in place of the butter.*

STORAGE INSTRUCTIONS: *Just like the shortbread crust, you can easily make this crust a day or two ahead and store it in the fridge. Just be sure to shape it into the pan for your intended recipe and wrap it tightly in plastic wrap so it doesn't dry out too much. You can bake it straight from the fridge. You can also freeze it for several weeks, but be sure to let it thaw before baking.*

SWEETENER OPTIONS:
I find that this crust works best with a powdered bulk sweetener. If you use a non-bulk sweetener, you may need to add an extra tablespoon or two of almond flour to make up for the bulk. Do not use a granulated sweetener; it would be too gritty in this no-bake application.

NUTRITIONAL INFORMATION (crust only):

CALORIES: 126 | FAT: 11.6g | PROTEIN: 3.5g | CARBS: 4.3g | FIBER: 2.3g | ERYTHRITOL: 6g

WHIPPED CREAM

Yield: About 2 cups (¼ cup per serving)

Prep Time: 5 minutes

Cook Time: —

Back in my grad school days, a friend came over for Thanksgiving and watched in astonishment as I whipped cream for the pumpkin pie. She didn't know that whipped cream didn't have to come from a can! There is nothing in the world quite like freshly whipped, lightly sweetened whipped cream. It's great as a dessert topping, of course, but if you choose to dig in with a spoon, I am not one to judge.

1 cup heavy whipping cream

2 tablespoons powdered erythritol-based sweetener

½ teaspoon vanilla extract

In a large mixing bowl, beat the cream, sweetener, and vanilla extract with an electric mixer until it holds stiff peaks.

SWEETENER OPTIONS: I find that my whipped cream holds better when I use a powdered bulk sweetener, but you can use any non-bulk sweetener.

TIP: *I like my whipped cream less sweet, especially when I am using fresh organic cream that doesn't contain any fillers or gums. If you prefer it sweeter, add another tablespoon of powdered sweetener.*

STORAGE INSTRUCTIONS: *Keep refrigerated until ready to use. This whipped cream will keep for as long as your cream normally would, but it tends to reliquefy after a day or two in the fridge.*

NUTRITIONAL INFORMATION

CALORIES: 104 | FAT: 10.4g | PROTEIN: 0.6g | CARBS: 0.9g | FIBER: 0g | ERYTHRITOL: 3.8g

STABILIZED WHIPPED CREAM

Sometimes whipped cream starts to turn back to a liquid when it sits around too long. If you need it to last for a few days, try this stabilized version. It will hold its shape for up to a week and is great for frosting or topping your favorite desserts.

In a small bowl, whisk together 1 tablespoon of water with ½ teaspoon of grass-fed gelatin. Gently warm in the microwave and whisk until the gelatin dissolves. Begin whipping the cream, sweetener, and vanilla extract and slowly pour in the gelatin mixture. Whip until the cream holds stiff peaks.

COCONUT WHIPPED CREAM

Yield: About 1 cup (¼ cup per serving)
Prep Time: 8 minutes, plus time to chill milk, bowl, and beaters
Cook Time: —

1 (13.5-ounce) can full-fat coconut milk, chilled overnight

2 tablespoons powdered erythritol-based sweetener

½ teaspoon coconut or vanilla extract

SWEETENER OPTIONS:
Any sweetener will do here.

Coconut whipped cream is a fabulous dairy-free alternative to the real thing. It rocks its own special coconut flavor, and I like to bring that out even more by adding a little coconut extract. The trick is to chill the can of coconut milk for at least eight hours, if not more; it won't whip properly when it's warm.

1. Chill a mixing bowl and beaters in the fridge for at least 10 to 15 minutes.

2. Skim the solid portion (or coconut cream) of the coconut milk from the top of the can into the chilled mixing bowl. Discard the thinner coconut water or reserve it for another use. Beat the coconut cream with an electric mixer until it is smooth and light and holds soft peaks.

3. Add the sweetener and coconut extract and beat until just combined. Refrigerate until ready to use. The whipped cream will firm up in the refrigerator, so be sure to let it warm a bit on the counter before serving.

STORAGE INSTRUCTIONS: *Keep refrigerated until ready to use. This whipped cream will keep for as long as your coconut milk is good, up to 2 weeks.*

NUTRITIONAL INFORMATION
CALORIES: 184 | FAT: 18.5g | PROTEIN: 1.9g | CARBS: 2.7g | FIBER: 0g | ERYTHRITOL: 7.5g

CHOCOLATE BUTTERCREAM FROSTING

Yield: About 2½ cups (3 rounded tablespoons per serving)
Prep Time: 10 minutes
Cook Time: —

Yes, yes, I know that buttercream isn't supposed to be made with cream cheese. But here's the deal: conventional frostings require an insane amount of powdered sugar to give them the right consistency. I just don't like things that sweet anymore, and powdered sugar alternatives are very expensive. Using a little cream cheese gives this frosting some structure without adding 2 or 3 cups of powdered sweetener.

2 ounces unsweetened chocolate, chopped

1 tablespoon coconut oil

½ cup (1 stick) unsalted butter, softened

3 ounces cream cheese (¼ cup plus 2 tablespoons), softened

⅔ cup powdered erythritol-based sweetener

2 tablespoons cocoa powder

½ teaspoon vanilla extract

¼ to ½ cup heavy whipping cream, room temperature

1. In a medium microwave-safe bowl, combine the chocolate and coconut oil. Microwave in 30-second increments, stirring after each increment, until melted and smooth. Alternatively, you can melt the chocolate and coconut oil in a heatproof bowl set over a pan of barely simmering water. Set aside to cool to lukewarm.

2. In a large bowl, beat the butter and cream cheese until smooth. Beat in the sweetener and cocoa powder until well combined.

3. Add the melted chocolate and vanilla extract and beat until smooth. The mixture will be very thick at this point.

4. Add the cream a couple of tablespoons at a time until a spreadable consistency is achieved.

SWEETENER OPTIONS: A powdered bulk sweetener provides structure for a proper frosting, so it's the best option here.

SERVING SUGGESTION: *Spread this frosting over the One-Bowl Brownies (page 86) for an out-of-this-world chocolate experience. You can also make fun little sandwich cookies with the Slice-and-Bake Vanilla Wafers (page 60). If you need a quick birthday cake, try making one of the low-carb cake mixes from Swerve or Good Dee's and pairing it with this delicious buttercream.*

STORAGE INSTRUCTIONS: *This buttercream will last for up to a week in the fridge, but it really has the best consistency and is easiest to spread when made fresh.*

TIP: *This recipe makes enough frosting for 12 cupcakes or one 8-inch single-layer cake.*

NUTRITIONAL INFORMATION
CALORIES: 161 | FAT: 15.2g | PROTEIN: 1.6g | CARBS: 2.5g | FIBER: 1.1g | ERYTHRITOL: 13.7g

HOMEMADE CHOCOLATE
HAZELNUT SPREAD

Yield: ¾ cup (2 tablespoons per serving)
Prep Time: 10 minutes (not including time to toast and husk hazelnuts)
Cook Time: —

¾ cup hazelnuts, toasted and husked (see Tips)

2 to 3 tablespoons coconut oil, melted

2 tablespoons cocoa powder

2 tablespoons powdered erythritol-based sweetener

½ teaspoon vanilla extract

Pinch of salt

I wish you could see how often I make this Nutella-like spread. My kids love it and eat it with their low-carb muffins almost every morning. I like to use it in other desserts, and I have to fend the kids off or hide the jar if I want any!

1. In a food processor or high-powered blender, process the hazelnuts until they are finely ground and beginning to clump together.

2. Add 2 tablespoons of the coconut oil and continue to process until you have a smooth butter. Add the cocoa powder, sweetener, vanilla extract, and salt and blend until well combined. The mixture should be a little liquid-y. If it is very thick, add the remaining tablespoon of oil.

SWEETENER OPTIONS: A powdered bulk sweetener helps thicken this spread, but really any sweetener will do.

STORAGE INSTRUCTIONS: *This spread will last and last in the refrigerator, because there's nothing about it that will go bad. But you won't be able to keep it around that long! It will firm up in the fridge but will return to more liquid-y state at room temperature.*

TIPS: *If you have a Trader Joe's near you, they sell pre-roasted and husked unsalted hazelnuts. Total lifesaver—I buy four bags at a time! And there are other brands online as well. If you have to roast and husk your own hazelnuts, I find that the best way is to rub the toasted nuts between my fingers until most of the skin falls off. You will never get them completely free of husks, so don't worry too much about that.*

You can use another oil in place of the coconut oil, but I find that coconut oil makes it a little less liquid-y at room temperature than a liquid oil. How smooth you can get your chocolate hazelnut spread really depends on the quality of your food processor or blender.

NUTRITIONAL INFORMATION
CALORIES: 158 | FAT: 18.2g | PROTEIN: 3.3g | CARBS: 4.7g | FIBER: 2.7g | ERYTHRITOL: 5g

CARAMEL SAUCE

Yield: About 1 cup (2 tablespoons per serving)
Prep Time: 5 minutes
Cook Time: 10 minutes

¼ cup (½ stick) unsalted butter

¼ cup plus 2 tablespoons granulated erythritol-based sweetener

2 teaspoons yacón syrup (optional)

½ cup heavy whipping cream

¼ teaspoon xanthan gum

¼ teaspoon kosher or medium-grind sea salt

2 tablespoons water

I spent a long time developing a low-carb caramel sauce that I could feel really good about. This one checks every box for me—flavor, color, consistency, and nutrition.

1. In a medium saucepan over medium heat, melt the butter with the sweetener and yacón syrup, if using, stirring until the sweetener dissolves. Bring to a boil, then continue to boil for 3 to 5 minutes, until the color deepens.

2. Remove from the heat and add the cream. The mixture will bubble vigorously. Sprinkle with the xanthan gum and whisk vigorously to combine. Then add the salt.

3. Return the mixture to medium heat and boil for 1 more minute. Let cool to lukewarm, then stir in the water until well combined.

SWEETENER OPTIONS: Granulated erythritol or a granulated erythritol-based blend is one of the few sugar substitutes that actually caramelizes, so it's your only option for this recipe.

STORAGE INSTRUCTIONS: *This sauce can be stored in the fridge for up to a week or so. (I've actually stored mine for several weeks.) Just gently reheat it in the microwave or in a saucepan to make it pourable again.*

TIP: *You can skip the yacón syrup, but your sauce will have more caramel flavor and color if you include it. You can also use blackstrap molasses in its stead. Both yacón syrup and blackstrap molasses add only about 1 gram of carbs per serving.*

NUTRITIONAL INFORMATION
CALORIES: 113 | FAT: 10.8g | PROTEIN: 0.4g | CARBS: 3.4g | FIBER: 0g | ERYTHRITOL: 11.3g

SALTED CARAMEL
SAUCE

Simply stir in another ½
teaspoon of salt at the very end.

CHOCOLATE PEANUT BUTTER SAUCE FOR TWO

OPTION

Yield: About ¼ cup (2 tablespoons per serving)
Prep Time: 1 minute
Cook Time: 1 minute

2 tablespoons creamy peanut butter (salted)

1½ tablespoons unsalted butter

1 tablespoon powdered erythritol-based sweetener, plus more if desired

2 teaspoons cocoa powder

⅛ teaspoon vanilla extract

SWEETENER OPTIONS: Feel free to sweeten this sauce with whichever sweetener you like best.

DAIRY-FREE OPTION: *Use coconut oil in place of the butter.*

I love low-carb vanilla ice cream because it's a blank slate, just begging you to add your favorite toppings and sauces. This easy chocolate sauce answers that call, and you can always make a half batch for just one person.

1. Combine the peanut butter and butter in a microwave-safe bowl and microwave on high power until melted. Stir until smooth.

2. Whisk in the sweetener, cocoa powder, and vanilla extract. Taste and add more sweetener, if desired.

NUTRITIONAL INFORMATION
CALORIES: 177 | FAT: 15.9g | PROTEIN: 4g | CARBS: 4.6g | FIBER: 1.5g | ERYTHRITOL: 7.5g

COCONUT SPRINKLES

Yield: 1 tablespoon (1 teaspoon per serving)
Prep Time: 1 minute
Cook Time: —

1 tablespoon unsweetened shredded coconut

Natural food coloring in color of choice

STORAGE INSTRUCTIONS:
These sprinkles keep almost indefinitely, as long as your coconut is good. I have a little jar of the mixed colors in my baking cupboard, ready to use whenever I want fun sprinkles!

Using colored shredded coconut as sprinkles is a stroke of genius that my friends at Keto Kookie told me about. I had to try it myself, and I admit it's a pretty smart idea. It gives keto desserts a little festive flair.

1. In a small bowl, mix the shredded coconut with just a drop or two of the food coloring until well combined. If you are using powdered food coloring, add a drop of water to help the color adhere to the coconut.

2. Let dry until ready to use. Repeat with more coconut for any other colors of sprinkles you want.

CHOCOLATE DESSERT CUPS

Yield: 12 cups (2 per serving)
Prep Time: 15 minutes
Cook Time: 2 minutes
Inactive Time: 40 minutes

2 ounces sugar-free dark chocolate, chopped

¼ ounce cacao butter, or 1½ teaspoons coconut oil

These little chocolate cups add instant elegance to creamy keto dessert recipes. Add pudding or mousse, or just fill them with Whipped Cream (page 164) and top each cup with a berry. They are perfect little bite-size desserts.

1. Set 12 mini silicone or parchment paper liners in a mini muffin pan.

2. Place the chocolate and cacao butter in a microwave-safe bowl. Microwave on high power in 30-second increments, stirring after each increment, until melted and smooth. Alternatively, you can melt the chocolate and cacao butter together in a heatproof bowl set over a pan of barely simmering water.

3. Spoon about 1 teaspoon of the melted chocolate into each mini muffin liner and use the back of a spoon to coat the bottom and sides evenly. You should have some chocolate remaining.

4. Refrigerate the cups for 10 minutes, then use the remaining chocolate to recoat the sides and cover any thin parts. Refrigerate for about 30 minutes until completely set.

5. Gently peel away the muffin liners.

STORAGE INSTRUCTIONS: *These cups will last for weeks in the fridge, ready to use whenever you want them.*

TIPS: *I like using silicone liners for these cups, as they peel off quite nicely. I pinch the bottom part of the cup with my thumb on the inside and my forefinger on the outside. Then I peel the liner away gently with my other hand.*

You can also make regular muffin-size cups, but you will get only four of them, thus the carb count will be a little higher per serving.

NUTRITIONAL INFORMATION
CALORIES: 48 | FAT: 4.7g | PROTEIN: 0.5g | CARBS: 3.8g | FIBER: 1.9g | ERYTHRITOL: 2g

APPENDIX: HOW TO RESCUE ALMOST ANYTHING

Words cannot express how much it pains me when someone says a recipe didn't turn out, so they threw it all away. Please don't do this. Stop and think. These ingredients are expensive, and there is a way to rescue almost anything. It may not be the dessert you had in mind, but it can still be wonderful. It might even be better than the original! You just have to think a little outside the box.

The cake broke coming out of the pan. It happens to the best of us, my friend. If it breaks into two or three pieces, you can sometimes patch it back together and frost or glaze it, and no one will be the wiser. However, if it's really a mess, then there are a few things you can do with it:

- **Cake truffles:** Crumble it all up, add some melted butter, smoosh it together, and roll it into balls. Bonus points for dipping the balls in chocolate. Kids love this kind of treat!

- **Trifle or parfaits:** Crumble the cake into big pieces and layer them with whipped cream or pudding. You can do one big trifle or smaller individual-size parfaits.

Your cake deflated. This can happen for any number of reasons, including old baking powder or not baking the cake long enough. Turn it into a positive by filling that hole with berries and whipped cream. People might even think you meant to do it.

The bottoms of your cookies burned. Scrape off the tops and turn them into truffles, parfaits, or sundaes. Who's going to say no to some crumbled cookies on their ice cream? I certainly won't!

The filling didn't set properly. So many variables can go into puddings and other creamy desserts that sometimes they don't want to set. Rather than serve a gooey mess, just pop the whole thing in the freezer and turn it into a tasty frozen dessert.

The filling curdled. Cooking with eggs can be tricky; apply a little too much heat for too long and suddenly you've got something akin to sweetened scrambled eggs. All is not lost! Get it off the heat as quickly as possible and transfer it to a blender to smooth it out again.

Your chocolate seized. There you are, going along nicely with your melted chocolate, and then suddenly it becomes a weird gloppy mess. It's incredibly frustrating. But even if it seems like it's destined for the trash bin, it's worth a shot to try to save it. Keep the chocolate over low heat and add more liquid, like water, 1 tablespoon at a time, whisking constantly. This doesn't always work, but often the chocolate will become smooth again.

All that being said, if you accidentally used salt instead of sweetener or made some other crazy mistake, you may need to chuck your dessert. And then head straight to your kitchen and make sure all of your containers are properly labeled!

RECIPE INDEX

CHAPTER 1: Candies and Confections

CHAPTER 2: Cookies

CHAPTER 3: Bars

78

No-Bake Chocolate "Oatmeal" Bars

80

Sugar Cookie Bars

82

Dairy-Free Peanut Butter Bars

84

No-Bake Blueberry Cheesecake Bars

86

One-Bowl Brownies

88

Dairy-Free Coconut Bars

90

No-Bake French Silk Pie Bars

CHAPTER 4: Cakes

94

Mini No-Bake Lemon Cheesecakes

96

Tiramisu Sheet Cake

98

Slow Cooker Chocolate Cake

100

Funfetti Mug Cakes

102

Dutch Butter Cake

104

Orange Cardamom Bundt Cake

106

Pumpkin Spice Mug Cakes

CHAPTER 5: Pies and Tarts

110
Mocha Cream Pie

112
Coconut Custard Pie

114
Lemon Curd Tartlets

116
Dairy-Free Fruit Tarts

118
Chocolate Hazelnut Brownie Pie

120
Strawberry Rhubarb Crisp for Two

CHAPTER 6: Frozen Desserts

124
Vanilla Bean Semifreddo

126
Salted Caramel Affogato

127
Ridiculously Easy Root Beer Floats

128
Chocolate Fat Bomb Ice Cream

130
Frozen Key Lime Mini Pies

132
Strawberry Cheesecake Pops

134
Coconut Milk Fudge Pops

CHAPTER 7: Custard, Mousse, and Other Delicious Desserts

138
Butterscotch Pudding

140
Dairy-Free
Peanut Butter Mousse

142
Mascarpone Mousse
with Roasted
Strawberries

144
Chocolate Hazelnut
Mousse

146
Lemon Curd Mousse

148
Raspberry Fool

150
Cannoli Dessert Dip

152
Slow Cooker
Coffee Coconut
Custard

154
Coconut Lime
Panna Cotta

156
Chocolate Cobbler

CHAPTER 8: Extras

160
Easy Shortbread Crust

162
Easy Chocolate
Pie Crust

164
Whipped Cream

166
Coconut
Whipped Cream

168
Chocolate
Buttercream Frosting

170
Homemade Chocolate
Hazelnut Spread

172
Caramel Sauce

174
Chocolate Peanut
Butter Sauce for Two

175
Coconut Sprinkles

176
Chocolate
Dessert Cups

RECIPE QUICK REFERENCE

RECIPES	PAGE	⊘	⊘	⊘	⊞	❄	🧁	👥	🌀
Peppermint Patties	44	✓	✓	✓	✓	✓		✓	
Chocolate-Covered Cheesecake Bites	46		✓	✓	✓	✓		✓	
Maple Walnut Fudge Cups	48		✓		✓	✓		✓	
Toffee Almond Bark	50		✓		✓			✓	
Macadamia Coconut Truffles	52	✓	✓		✓	✓		✓	
Peanut Butter and Jam Cups	54	✓	✓	✓	✓			✓	
Watermelon Lime Gummies	56	✓	✓	✓	✓				
Slice-and-Bake Vanilla Wafers	60		✓			✓		✓	
Amaretti	62	✓							
Peanut Butter Cookies for Two	64	O		✓			✓		✓
Cream Cheese Cookies	66					✓		✓	✓
Chewy Double Chocolate Cookies	68	O				✓			✓
No-Bake Peanut Butter Caramel Cookies	70		✓		✓			✓	
Chocolate Hazelnut Thumbprints	72	O						✓	
Deep-Dish Chocolate Chip Cookies	74	O					✓		✓
No-Bake Chocolate "Oatmeal" Bars	78		✓		✓	✓		✓	
Sugar Cookie Bars	80							✓	
Dairy-Free Peanut Butter Bars	82	✓	✓	✓	✓			✓	
No-Bake Blueberry Cheesecake Bars	84		✓		✓			✓	
One-Bowl Brownies	86	✓						✓	✓
Dairy-Free Coconut Bars	88	✓	✓	✓	✓			✓	
No-Bake French Silk Pie Bars	90					✓		✓	
Mini No-Bake Lemon Cheesecakes	94		✓		✓	✓			
Tiramisu Sheet Cake	96							✓	
Slow Cooker Chocolate Cake	98	O							
Funfetti Mug Cakes	100	O					✓		✓
Dutch Butter Cake	102								
Orange Cardamom Bundt Cake	104	✓				✓		✓	
Pumpkin Spice Mug Cakes	106	✓		✓			✓		✓
Mocha Cream Pie	110		✓		✓	✓			
Coconut Custard Pie	112	O		✓					

RECIPES	PAGE								
Lemon Curd Tartlets	114							✓	
Dairy-Free Fruit Tarts	116	✓	✓		✓		✓		
Chocolate Hazelnut Brownie Pie	118	O				✓			
Strawberry Rhubarb Crisp for Two	120	O	✓				✓		✓
Vanilla Bean Semifreddo	124			✓	✓	✓			
Salted Caramel Affogato	126			✓	✓		✓		
Ridiculously Easy Root Beer Floats	127	O	✓	✓	✓		✓		
Chocolate Fat Bomb Ice Cream	128		✓	✓	✓	✓			
Frozen Key Lime Mini Pies	130		✓		✓	✓			
Strawberry Cheesecake Pops	132	O	✓	✓	✓	✓			
Coconut Milk Fudge Pops	134	✓	✓	✓	✓	✓			
Butterscotch Pudding	138			O	✓				
Dairy-Free Peanut Butter Mousse	140	✓	✓	✓	✓				
Mascarpone Mousse with Roasted Strawberries	142		✓	✓					✓
Chocolate Hazelnut Mousse	144		✓		✓				✓
Lemon Curd Mousse	146			✓			✓		
Raspberry Fool	148	O	✓	✓	✓		✓		✓
Cannoli Dessert Dip	150		✓	✓	✓				✓
Slow Cooker Coffee Coconut Custard	152	✓		✓	✓		✓		
Coconut Lime Panna Cotta	154	✓	✓	✓			✓		
Chocolate Cobbler	156	O	✓						
Easy Shortbread Crust	160	O	✓		✓	✓			✓
Easy Chocolate Pie Crust	162	O	✓		✓	✓			✓
Whipped Cream	164		✓	✓	✓				✓
Coconut Whipped Cream	166	✓	✓	✓	✓		✓		✓
Chocolate Buttercream Frosting	168		✓	✓	✓			✓	✓
Homemade Chocolate Hazelnut Spread	170	✓	✓		✓				✓
Caramel Sauce	172		✓	✓	✓				✓
Chocolate Peanut Butter Sauce for Two	174	O	✓	✓	✓		✓		✓
Coconut Sprinkles	175	✓	✓	✓	✓		✓		✓
Chocolate Dessert Cups	176	✓	✓	✓	✓				

GENERAL INDEX